JESUS

HIS CHURCH AND ITS MISSION

A Deeper Look into the Character and Nature of the Church and God's Intentions for It

David L. Tice

1

Scriptures marked ESV are taken from the THE HOLY BIBLE, ENGLISH STANDARD VERSION (ESV): Scriptures taken from THE HOLY BIBLE, ENGLISH STANDARD VERSION ® Copyright© 2001 by Crossway, a publishing ministry of Good News Publishers. Used by permission.

Scriptures marked TLB are taken from the THE LIVING BIBLE (TLB): Scripture taken from THE LIVING BIBLE copyright© 1971. Used by permission of Tyndale House Publishers, Inc., Carol Stream, Illinois 60188. All rights reserved.

Scriptures marked TMB are taken from the THE MESSAGE: THE BIBLE IN CONTEMPORARY ENGLISH (TM): copyright©1993, 1994, 1995, 1996, 2000, 2001, 2002. Used by permission of NavPress Publishing Group

A few journalistic observations:

Quotes from Strong's, Vine's, Bible dictionaries, Interlinear Bibles, etc. have been edited (no words were changed) to help with clarity as well as for conciseness. I have not attempted to modernize grammar in quotes or to change spelling or capitalization; they remain as they were written.

Any <u>underlined</u> or **bolded** words in quoted material has been added by me to emphasize a word or point.

Church is capitalized on purpose throughout this book when it refers to God's people. As God's family, as His chosen people, as those who He loves so much that He was willing to die for, capitalizing the name is the least I can do to honor them.

Satan's name, other than as the first word of a sentence, is not capitalized because I do not wish to give him any honor at all.

I have included questions at the end of each chapter that can be used in a small group Bible study setting.

In this book I will be using the terms: servant, child, friend, brother, son and bride. These different terms can speak of changes and/or growth in our relationship with God but they can also speak of different aspects of our relationship with God. If I get excited about sons of God, I am excited about the relationship that this phrase implies: being like our Father, being about the Father's business, being trained and loved by our Father, carrying our Father's DNA. When I get excited about the bride of Christ, I am excited about the relationship that this phrase implies; a man's love for his bride is different than his love for his son. Both types of love are awesome and I think we can enjoy both kinds of love from God. The bride of Christ also opens the door to an intimacy with God that a brother or son just does not have. I am not speaking here of anything sensual or sexual, I am speaking of intimacy that produces a new kind of life in the recipient of that love. I share this so that you won't focus on the terms as much as the symbolism they represent.

DEDICATION

First of all, this book is dedicated to the Lord Jesus Christ, without Whom we wouldn't even be concerned with pursuing Spiritual truths.

Then to my wife, Lillian, who has faithfully served the Lord with me throughout our marriage. Our marriage is truly a match made in heaven.

Also, to my mother, Lillie Mae Tice, for her fervent prayers and hunger for the Lord. Among my most precious memories are the times I would come home from school and call out, "Mom, I'm home!" I would then listen for her reply, but many times what I heard was her voice coming from the back of the house speaking to the Lord fervently in prayer. She is an example of someone who desires the "meat of the Word" as she pursues a deeper relationship with God.

ACKNOWLEDGMENTS

I would like to thank a number of people for their help in getting this book to press. First of all, thanks to Lanette Smith and Mrs. Barbara Jacobs for helping me by proofreading many manuscripts that preceded this finished copy. This book could not have progressed to a comprehensible state without your help. Also, I would like to thank Lillian Tice, Katherine Grove, Susan Perkins and Hannah Cook who inspired many rewrites and assisted in numerous ways to help this book come to completion. And David Smith, what's a book without a cover? Thank you for the cover design and the drawings of the furniture in the Tabernacle. I also want to acknowledge those whose lives have influenced me in my Christian walk throughout my life.

For the inspiration to write this book, I give the glory to God! I struggled with the concept of being a writer; I am a preacher and have done that for many years; could I shift that into the arena of the written word? I hope I did. My prayer is that the message that God put on my heart unfolds in an understandable way in this book.

Any errors that still remain are mine and mine alone. Those who helped me had to work with what I gave them.

May God bless you and quicken to your understanding His message in this book.

David L. Tice

TABLE OF CONTENTS

INTRODUCTION

I love God's Church. I grew up in Church. The earliest memories that I have are of events at church. I was saved at an early age (probably around 6 or 8 years old) and throughout my whole life I have heard people say that they attended or were building a New Testament Church. As I got older and grew in some knowledge of the Bible, I would wonder, "What does that mean?" Aren't ALL churches New Testament Churches since the Church did not exist before Jesus' death and resurrection? (See note at the end of the introduction.) Or, I would wonder, "Is your Church like the one at Corinth, or the one at Jerusalem, or one of those described in Revelation chapters 1-3?" What is a New Testament Church supposed to look like?

Early in my adult life, God called me into full-time ministry and my questions about the Church shifted from curiosity to genuine questions I needed to consider as I worked to build this type of Church. My wife and I moved to Springfield, Missouri, to attend a Church called House of Prayer. After a few years as a part of the leadership of that Church, I was asked to be an associate pastor. A few years before the founding pastor (Bill Britton) went on to his reward in Heaven, I was set in as the full-time pastor. More than 40 years later, I'm still pastoring and during those years I continued to wonder about the nature of the New Testament Church.

In my meditation on Jesus' Church, some of the first things that were clear were what the Church does NOT have. The Church does not have a special priesthood; we are all priests unto God. A person's role in the Church is not determined by what tribe you are a part of (your lineage).The Church does not have special garments for those who lead, and so on. In other words, the Church is not like the pattern given to Moses at all. It appears that Jesus was thinking about this change when He said: "No one sews a piece of unshrunk cloth on an old garment; or else the new piece pulls away from the old, and the tear is made worse. And no one puts new wine into old wineskins; or else the new wine bursts the wineskins, the wine is spilled, and the wineskins are ruined. But new wine must be put into new wineskins." (Mark 2:21–22) When the New

Testament churches were founded, the functioning of the Church was unprecedented; no one knew what it was supposed to be like or how it was supposed to operate. As I realized Jesus was calling for a completely new design, I turned to Jesus' words for more guidance.

Jesus spoke specifically of the Church only twice, once in Matthew 16:17-19 and the other time in Matthew 18:15-20. As a pastor I have preached using these passages of Scripture many times and considered them to be about Jesus' promise to build "His" Church and that in this future Church, we should work to keep peace between God's people. I know there are other things to be considered in those passages but this is what would come to mind when I considered what Jesus had to say about His Church. Over the years, that first passage has greatly encouraged me, as a pastor, knowing that it was not on my shoulders to build God's Church but that Jesus was at work all the time building His Church.

So, rather than specific logistical instructions such as structure and new roles, Jesus' words gave principles to follow and reassurance that Jesus was always active in building the Church and the responsibility was not all on us humans. Still, I desired more specific instructions. For those, I looked at the rest of the New Testament and couldn't see the forest for the trees. In the Book of Acts, there were so many different things going on in different churches that I couldn't find a clear New Testament Church pattern. In the Old Testament, God showed Moses on the mountain exactly what the Tabernacle was supposed to look like. Then God told Moses when he was getting ready to build the Tabernacle, "And see to it that you make them according to the pattern which was shown you on the mountain...." (Exodus 25:40) The clarity of the Old Testament pattern caused me to cry out to God, "Where is Your pattern for the New Testament Church?"

Something in me kept looking for a clearer picture but I struggled to find it. The Word of God says, "But the path of the just is like the shining sun, that shines ever brighter unto the perfect day." (Proverbs 4:18) So, shouldn't it be even clearer under the New Covenant what God wants His Church to be? Because I could not see a clear pattern for the Church that Jesus was building, I didn't have a clear vision of how to lead the people I was called to pastor. It was difficult to build something when I didn't have a clear picture of what it should be like. It was kind of like Yogi Berra's famous quote: "If you don't know where you are going, you'll end up someplace else."

Then just recently, I read "Growing Strong Churches" by Bill Scheidler. He opened my eyes to see that what Jesus said to Peter about Jesus building His Church was not just an encouragement to pastors that Jesus was in charge, but that in that passage of Scripture (Matthew 18) the very nature of this future Church was being disclosed. He also went into the passage about dealing with problems in the Church and again his writing opened my eyes to see the nature of this future Church. Then he went into the Book of Acts and showed universal traits of the Church. Wow! What insight! So, as I began a search through the Gospels to see what else I could find, I came across more that I realized was revealed about His Church through the words of Jesus.

I am sure I have not discovered all that is hidden in the New Testament about a "pattern" for the New Testament Church. I have not tried to apply the parables, or the Sermon on the Mount, or many other wonderful things that Jesus said that can be applied to our lives today. I limited myself to what seemed rather obvious (after the window of insight was thrown open). I looked for traits that applied directly to the nature and/or character of the Church, focusing on those traits that should be a part of that wonderful, glorious future Church.

> *"God does not conceal a matter to keep it hidden from us, but that His Spirit might reveal it to us in His time."*

I pray that this book will stir your heart to search out more of the "unsearchable" truths concerning the New Testament Church that are hidden in God's Word. "It is the glory of God to conceal a matter, but the glory of kings is to search out a matter." (Proverbs 25:2) Bill Johnson once said, "God does not conceal a matter to keep it hidden from us, but that His Spirit might reveal it to us in His time." (Luke 10:21; John 14:26)

Before I delve into sharing information about the Church, please listen to this strong warning: I do not believe that the traits discovered in Jesus' teachings and unfolded in the Church in Acts should become a new form of legalism. These traits cannot be forced upon people, they come from within. However, since these traits are supposed to be in the Church, we need to encourage their growth and development. For example, if we realize that one of the traits of the Church is brotherly love, we will encourage and help develop loving relationships in our own lives as well as among Church members.

One very important facet about these traits must be considered. As a pastor, I have often counseled young married couples and have realized that unvoiced expectations can really place a strain on a marriage. For example, suppose the wife has been raised in a home where the father always kept the trash can emptied without it ever needing to be brought to his attention. The house would always be trash free and that is what the wife would automatically expect in her home without even thinking about it. Now, suppose the husband has been raised in a home where the trash can would fill up and overflow. No one took the responsibility to empty the trash can. In that home whenever it got so bad that the wife couldn't handle it anymore she would yell at her husband to please take the trash out of the house. Maybe they would argue back and forth a few times before it finally got cleaned up but when the wife got upset enough the husband would begrudgingly carry it out. How is the newly married couple going to deal with trash in the house? This kind of problem is not something that is usually talked about before marriage so here is my take on what could happen. The trash can runs over, the wife gets frustrated and begins to feel like her husband doesn't love her and she may not even know why she feels this way. The husband is oblivious. Everything is great as far as he is concerned and he cannot understand why his wife is upset. Finally, the wife blows up and screams that she cannot stand it with trash overflowing the trash can and the husband thinks, "What's the big deal?" This scenario might not be the way you would show an unvoiced expectation, but you can get the picture. Many of God's expectations are as clear as the Ten Commandments, but others are a little more challenging to find.

I don't believe God has unvoiced expectations. His expectations are clearly revealed in His Word. What I believe is that we have not known to search them out and as a result we have not recognized many things that God expects from us as His Church and as individual Christians.

I want to point out that my expected audience for this book is the Church in the United States of America. I was born here and have lived my life here and this is where I will first release this book. My examples come from my life and experience in the United States. It is not my contention that the culture of the United States is superior in any way to other cultures around the world. I love the cultural differences that I have been introduced to as I have had opportunity to travel outside the U.S., but I grew up in and I live in the U.S., and its culture pervades my life. I do believe that the culture of the Kingdom of God is superior to all other cultures. Jesus said, "But seek first the kingdom of God and His righteousness...." (Matthew 6:33a) In this book, my goal is to exalt King Jesus and His kingdom and to bring us to live more closely in its culture.

SOME SUGGESTIONS AS YOU READ THIS BOOK:

- Pray and ask the Holy Spirit to reveal insights in the Word —after all He is the supreme teacher.
- Read with an open Bible nearby.
- Read with a highlighter in your hand.
- Don't skip the questions. If you are reading this book on your own, write your answers down. As you ponder each question, it will help "engraft" the Word of God into your heart. (James 1:21)
- Don't rush through the book. This book is not intended for easy reading, but rather to challenge you in your understanding and functioning as a viable member of the Body of Christ.

Note: Stephen called the people of Israel, as they left Egypt and were on their way to the Promised Land, "the church in the wilderness." (Acts 7:38) That has interesting implications and we will look at that in Part 2.

PART I

THE NATURE OF THE CHURCH

THE NATURE OF THE CHURCH

Throughout the last number of centuries we have considered the Church to be:

- the people of God;
- a place for the family of God to gather together and worship God;
- a place where we come together to grow in the knowledge of God;
- a place where we gather together to love one another;
- a place where the unsaved can hear the Good News and come to salvation;
- a place where we do all the things that Churches do.

The Church that Jesus is building is all of these things; however, the Church is supposed to be and do so much more than this.

> *Jesus sent His Church on a mission and it is not just to save souls, it is also the redemption of the whole creation.*

One important thought as we begin to look at Jesus' expectations for His Church is that Jesus gave us words of wisdom about the preparation needed in Luke 14:28–32. "For which of you, intending to build a tower, does not sit down first and count the cost, whether he has enough to finish it—lest, after he has laid the foundation, and is not able to finish, all who see it begin to mock him, saying, 'This man began to build and was not able to finish.' Or what king, going to make war against another king, does not sit down first and consider whether he is able with ten thousand to meet him who comes against him with twenty thousand? Or else, while the other is still a great way off, he sends a delegation and asks conditions of peace." The two parts of this Scripture accurately represent the different parts of this book. The first reference is to building a tower. This parallels Jesus building His Church which is the focus of Parts 1 and 2 of this book. The second part of the verse is about being in a war. (Here we are using the word war in a metaphorical way. Ephesians 6:12 says, "... we do not wrestle against flesh and blood, but against principalities, against powers, against the rulers of the darkness of this age, against spiritual hosts of wickedness in the heavenly places." We are looking at our struggle against satan and all his demonic forces.) Jesus' statement about going to war parallels the focus of Parts 3 and 4 of this book. Jesus sent His Church on a mission and it is not just to save souls, it is also the redemption of the whole of creation. (Romans 8:19-22)

Jesus expects us to succeed in His purpose of having a "glorious Church without spot or blemish...." (Ephesians 5:27) There is no "Plan B" in Heaven's play book. Jesus counted the cost before time began (Ephesians 1:4) and determined not only that we are worth the price He had to pay but that He would also give us "all things that pertain [are requisite and suited (AMP)] to life and godliness..." (2 Peter 1:3) so that we would be able to finish "the race set before us...." (Hebrews 12:1)

In Ephesians 3:9-11 (NLT) the Apostle Paul writes, "I was chosen to explain to everyone this mysterious plan that God, the Creator of all things, had kept secret from the beginning. God's purpose in all this was to use the Church to display His wisdom in its rich variety to all the unseen rulers and authorities in the heavenly places. This was his eternal plan, which he carried out through Christ Jesus our Lord." God did not set a low bar for His Church. God set the bar very high and He will have a Church that is able to measure up to His greatest expectations.

Remember Gabriel's words to Mary in Luke 1:37 "For with God nothing will be impossible." God, who out of nothing created everything that was created, is well able to bring us, His Church, into the fullness that He, before time began, has purposed for us.

> **God will have a Church that is able to measure up to His greatest expectations.**

THE ECCLESIA

Before we consider what Jesus said about the future Church, let's look at the meaning of the word He used. Jesus used this word in two different places. One time is Matthew 16:18. "And I also say to you that you are Peter, and on this rock I will build My church, and the gates of Hades shall not prevail against it." The other time is Matthew 18:17. "And if he refuses to hear them, tell it to the church. But if he refuses even to hear the church, let him be to you like a heathen and a tax collector." The word Jesus used for the Church was in common use in the Roman Empire but it had nothing to do with Church as we know it today.

> *The local Church, as referenced by Jesus Christ, is not only a place for people to come together for worship, preaching, and fellowship but it is also an assembly of believers who are to impact their geographical region.*

So, what is this mysterious word anyway? It is the Greek word ECCLESIA. In Christian circles the word ecclesia is usually translated as meaning the "called out ones." However, it is much more than that. The following is taken from the <u>International Dictionary of New Testament Theology.</u> Here we learn the common usage of ecclesia in the Greek and Roman culture of Jesus' day:

ECCLESIA: An assembly of competent citizens of a region who met at regular intervals to govern.

- *Deciding on suggested laws and final decisions (They couldn't suggest a new law.)*
- *Appointing individuals into official positions*
- *Summoning its army to assemble for war*
- *Developing both internal and external policies in the region including contracts, treaties, war and peace, and financial matters*
- *Voting in those who would sit at the Areopagus (similar to the Supreme Court of the United States of America)*
- *Ruling on societal and cultural matters for its territory*

The local Church, as referenced by Jesus Christ, is not only a place for people to come together for worship, preaching, and fellowship but it is also an assembly of believers who are to impact their geographical region. As the Universal and Local Church, we have been called by God Himself to pray, "...Our Father in heaven, Hallowed be Your name. Your kingdom come. Your will be done on earth as *it is* in heaven." (Matthew 6:9–10) This is the cry of God's heart for the world and Jesus' use of the word ecclesia to describe the Church indicates that the Church is His plan to bridge from the heavenly kingdom to earth.

Let us look at these areas one at a time and consider how Jesus might want His Church to fulfill the role of a Spiritual ecclesia. (I'm writing this as a person living in the United States of America, other parts of the world might need to adjust these thoughts somewhat to fit their own unique social, political, and economic situation.)

- **The ecclesia was an assembly of competent citizens of a region who met at regular intervals to govern.**

In 1975, Bill Bright, founder of Campus Crusade and Loren Cunningham, founder of Youth With a Mission (YWAM), developed a God-given, world-changing strategy. Their mandate: Bring Godly change to a nation by reaching its seven spheres, or mountains, of societal influence. They defined these mountains or spheres as: Arts and Entertainment, Business, Education, Family, Government, Media, and Religion. Over the centuries the Church had been involved in these areas of influence. Then a few decades ago there seemed to be a change and the Church became more self-focused. Recently there has been a renewed focus upon the Church getting involved once again in these mountains of influence. The reason these areas are so important is that they are the major culture change agents in most modern societies.

As a Christian young man growing up in the 1950s and 1960s, I remember hearing such statements as: "Stay out of politics, it's a dirty business." Or "Don't go to movies, Hollywood is immoral." Or "People don't talk about religion in polite society." Or "Don't become a lawyer; they're just money grubbing ambulance chasers."

> *The seven mountains or spheres of influence:*
> - *Arts and Entertainment*
> - *Business*
> - *Education*
> - *Family*
> - *Government*
> - *Media*
> - *Religion*

As a result of this kind of thinking, Evangelical and Pentecostal Christians withdrew from these areas and satan was able to move in. In a struggle, if you are in a contested territory and you walk away, you have just surrendered that territory to the enemy without a fight. I am not saying that there are no Christians in these areas of influence, but that Christians, in general, had stopped trying to influence them and pretty much surrendered these mountains to secular forces.

One day my youngest daughter was talking to a very intelligent fellow Christian who asked this question: "What would the ACLU be like today if most of the Christian lawyers had not left the organization?" What a powerful question! Think about this concept, not just as it pertains to the ACLU but to each of the seven mountains. How can we be salt and light if we are not there and we don't speak up? Maybe the ACLU would not be a nice, Christian organization, but it would definitely not be what it is today!

Consider the mountain of government. The Bible says, "When the righteous are in authority, the people rejoice; But when a wicked man rules, the people groan." (Proverbs 29:2) How are we going to have the righteous in authority if no Godly person is willing to get involved? The Church must not only vote for Godly standards and laws, but must be willing to run for office so that the Church has someone Godly to vote for. How often have you heard it said: "Well, I guess I'll vote for _____, he/she is the lesser of two evils."? How horrible it is that voting too often comes to that kind of a decision! We need to encourage young Christians that just as it is right and Godly for them to be pastors and missionaries, it is also right and Godly to run for office. Then when they do run for office, stand behind them with prayer and Godly council. If you are worried that they will be influenced by the evil in politics (and there is evil in politics), pray and ask God how to establish an accountability group to hold them up in prayer and then

> *In a struggle, if you are in a contested territory and you walk away, you have just surrendered that territory to the enemy without a fight.*

determine to meet with them on a regular basis to keep their walk in the Lord fresh and grounded. Look at how the Godly kings in the Old Testament affected the people and culture of Israel during their reigns. Don't we want that for our communities?

- **The ecclesia made decisions on suggested laws and final decisions**

They couldn't suggest a new law: we can.

I know that this is not true everywhere, but we in America have the opportunity to have an even greater influence on the laws in our regions than the ecclesia of old. We can become legislators and introduce those laws, or we can get petitions signed to put propositions on a ballot. We can even go so far as to amend our state constitutions. Are we using this power to make our city, county, state and nation a better place, or has our salt lost its savor (Matthew 5:13)?

- **The ecclesia made appointments to official positions.**

The Church is supposed to be involved in the governmental affairs of the city, county, state and nation, putting people into and taking them out of official positions. What a far cry from the message I heard as a child and young man: "Don't get involved in politics." However, to be effectively involved we need to be aware of who is doing a good job and who is abusing their position for personal or political gain. Many solid Christian and/or conservative organizations research proposed laws and candidates. Look for some in your area and make sure the information gets passed around. If there aren't any such organizations in your area, start one. Technology is a powerful tool. Do some research and share it with people in your area who are concerned about the issues facing your community.

- **The ecclesia was involved in both internal and external policies in the region including contracts, treaties, war and peace, and financial matters.**

How can the Church be involved in policies both internal and external to our regions of influence if we are not involved in government either by contacting those who are in our government or by getting involved in government ourselves?

> *The Church is supposed to be involved in governmental affairs.*

- **The ecclesia could summon its army to assemble for war.**

What about that idea of the Church going to war? Based on several Scriptures, I would say that we are already involved in warfare! BUT, this warfare is spiritual and not natural. Ephesians 6:12, "For we do not wrestle against flesh and blood, but against principalities, against powers, against the rulers of the darkness of this age, against spiritual *hosts* of wickedness in the heavenly places." And 2 Corinthians 10:3-5, "For though we walk in the flesh, we do not war according to the flesh. For the weapons of our warfare *are* not carnal but mighty in God for pulling down strongholds, casting down arguments and every high thing that exalts itself against the knowledge of God, bringing every thought into captivity to the obedience of Christ." These Scriptures explain that this war is spiritual and continuous.

> *The Church is designed to influence the societies in which we live rather than being influenced by the societies in which we live.*

Even though we are in a spiritual rather than physical war, this spiritual warfare has a very real impact on this earth. We as Christians must join together with other Christians to pray for our neighborhoods, cities, states, and our nation. Unlike physical wars, we know the outcome of this spiritual war. Remember, Jesus said of His Church, "the gates of Hades shall not prevail against it." (Matthew 16:18) The Church is Jesus' method and plan for winning the spiritual war.

- **Voted in those who would sit at the Areopagus**

In the United States, the Areopagus would be similar to the Supreme Court. In the United States, Christians have the opportunity to vote for or against local judges. We must make decisions based on Biblical standards and not on political affiliation.

- **The ecclesia ruled on societal and cultural matters for its territory.**

SOCIETAL – From Dictionary.com I got this definition: noting or pertaining to large social groups, or to their activities, customs, etc.

From Macmillandictionary.com societal is: relating to society or to the way society is organized.

Wikipedia says, "Culture is the social behavior and norms found in human societies." The Cambridge English Dictionary expands on that and states that culture is "the way of life, especially the general customs and beliefs, of a particular group of people at a particular time."

I once heard someone say, "The Church reflects changes in society; they are just a few years behind." Whether changes do or do not implement God's desires for the world, the idea that the church passively adopts whatever is happening in society is certainly not Jesus' vision for the Church. The Church is designed to influence the societies in which we live rather than being influenced by the societies in which we live. The Scripture declares: "And do not be conformed to this world, but be transformed by the renewing of your mind...." (Romans 12:2) We have to be careful to "not love the world or the things in the world. If anyone loves the world, the love of the Father is not in him." (1 John 2:15 KJV) (See chapter 13 "Work of the Apostle" for more on this.)

The Church of Jesus Christ is supposed to change, for the good, the world in which we live. I am not proposing that we start a new Christian political party. If you are a Democrat, be a Christian Democrat and stand up for Godly principles, ethics, moral values, etc. The same thing holds true if you are a Republican, a Libertarian, a Green Party or an Independent. We don't all have to join the same party, but we really must be salt and light in the party to which we belong.

I have been talking about Christians being salt and light in the world. Jesus said in Matthew 5:13–16, "You are the salt of the earth; but if the salt loses its flavor, how shall it be seasoned? It is then good for nothing but to be thrown out and trampled underfoot by men. You are the light of the world. A city that is set on a hill cannot be hidden. Nor do they light a lamp and put it under a basket, but on a lampstand, and it gives light to all who are in the house. Let your light so shine before men, that they may see your good works and glorify your Father in heaven." We all accept the reality that we are to be salt and light in this world. Salt and light affect everything with which they come in contact. Salt is both a

> *Salt and light affect everything with which they come in contact.*

flavor enhancer and a preserver but what we don't always think about is that salt is absolutely necessary for life. Without salt in our diets we will die. It is essential for the transfer of food and waste in and out of the cells in the human body.

Sunlight is a purifier; it purifies water as it flows down a mountainside. Sunlight is also the engine behind the earth's water cycle and sunlight is necessary for plants to grow. Without the effects of sunlight there would be no life on planet Earth. So should it be with the Church of Jesus Christ. His Church should be purifying and bringing life to the societies in which we live.

I heard someone say, "Revivals impact the Church but Great Awakenings impact society." A study through history shows how the Church impacted society during and immediately after the Great Awakenings of the past centuries. We need to be praying for and reaching for the next Great Awakening. God does not want us to settle for another revival. In fact if we do, we are being selfish and self-centered. What God wants is for His Church to be salt and light—agents of transformation in this world.

So, we know a little more about what the Church is supposed to do, but what is the Church like? What are the traits of this glorious entity that Jesus declared He would build? From the Old Testament we understand about priests, high priests, animal sacrifices, etc., and the parts they play in the worship of God under the Mosaic Covenant. And, we know the plan for the Church of the New Covenant is completely different. How do we go about doing Church in the New Covenant?

> *God wants His Church to be salt and light—*
> *agents of transformation in this world.*

How do you think your life should change knowing the true role of the ecclesia?

Are you familiar with the Great Awakenings? If so, what are some of the key elements that have been in each of the four Great Awakenings?

(If you are not familiar with the Great Awakenings, I would encourage you to do a little research and answer the previous question.)

Which of the Seven Mountains of Culture do you think has the greatest influence in your life?

Which of the Seven Mountains of Culture do you consider to be the greatest change agent in your culture?

Is there one of the Seven Mountains that you would like to get involved with to help redirect change in your city?

How will you go about getting involved and influencing your city?

How do you think your life would change?

DISCOVERING TRAITS
FROM JESUS' TEACHINGS

As I shared earlier, I longed for a greater understanding of the work and nature of the Church throughout my Christian experience. When my understanding was opened to see more clearly, wonderful insights into the Church of Jesus Christ began to unfold. In the following pages, I want to share what some of those insights are and how I arrived at them. Most of them are not new insights but here they are unveiled in an orderly fashion. As we contemplate the words of Jesus concerning the future Church, we get some insight into what that future Church is supposed to be like. This is not a picture of the way we are supposed to do Church as much as it is a picture of what the Church is in its nature and character.

As you read through the following pages, please don't get overwhelmed with lists and information. Some of this may be new to you but as you read this chapter, think about whether or not you and your fellow believers have these traits active in your lives and in the life of your local Church. Make this time not just a time of gathering information but a time of meditation on what God wants in the life of His Church.

In the following Scriptures, I believe Jesus' words are relating to the Universal Church.

Matthew 16:17-19 Jesus answered and said to him, "Blessed are you, Simon Bar-Jonah, for flesh and blood has not revealed this to you, but My Father who is in heaven. And I also say to you that you are Peter, and on this rock I will build My church, and the gates of Hades shall not prevail against it. And I will give you the keys of the kingdom of heaven, and whatever you bind on earth will be bound in heaven, and whatever you loose on earth will be loosed in heaven."

As we meditate on these Scriptures, important concepts begin to emerge:

Matthew 16:17-19 Jesus answered and said to him, "Blessed are you, Simon Bar-Jonah, for flesh and blood has not revealed this to you but My Father who is in heaven. *(The Church will be built on revelation from God.)*
And I also say to you that you are Peter, and on this rock *(The Church has a firm foundation.)*
I (Jesus Christ commissioned the Church.)
will build *(Jesus Christ will be the builder of the Church.)*
My church, *(The Church will belong to Jesus.)*
and the gates of Hades *(Satan is the enemy of the Church.)*
shall not prevail *(The Church will be a victorious church.)*
against it. *(The Church will be a unified church.)*
And I will give you the keys *(Jesus will give to the Church what it needs.)*
of the kingdom of heaven, *(The Church will be a Spiritual entity.)*
and whatever you bind *(The Church will have purpose.)*
on earth *(The Church will represent the authority of Christ on earth.)*
will be bound in heaven, *(God will hear and respond to the Church.)*
and whatever you loose on earth will be loosed in heaven." *(The Church will be proactive in its actions here on the earth so it will be a living, not stagnant entity.)*

In the following passage, it seems that Jesus is relating to an expression of the Local Church:

Matthew 18:15-20 "Moreover if your brother sins against you, go and tell him his fault between you and him alone. If he hears you, you have gained your brother. But if he will not hear, take with you one or two more, that 'by the mouth of two or three witnesses every word may be established.' And if he refuses to hear them, tell it to the church. But if he refuses even to hear the church, let him be to you like a heathen and a tax collector. Assuredly, I say to you, whatever you bind on earth will be bound in heaven, and whatever you loose on earth will be loosed in heaven. Again I say to you that if two of you agree on earth concerning anything that they ask, it will be done for them by My Father in heaven. For where two or three are gathered together in My name, I am there in the midst of them."

Again, important concepts come to light:

Matthew 18:15-20 Jesus said: "Moreover if your brother *(The Local Church will be a spiritual family.)*
sins against you, *(Until the Church is completed, there will be a great need for love, patience and a lot of forgiveness.)*
go *(The Local Church will be active.)*
and tell him his fault *(Members in a Local Church will not be perfect, but there will be accountability.)*
between you and him alone. *(Fellowship in faith and prayer will be found in the Local Church.)*
If he hears you, you have gained your brother. *(Jesus desires right relationships in His Church.)*
But if he will not hear, take with you one or two more, that 'by the mouth of two or three witnesses every word may be established.' *(The Local Church will have order.)*
And if he refuses them, tell it to the church. *(The Local Church will be a defined body of believers.)*
But if he refuses even to hear the church, let him be to you like a heathen and a tax collector. *(The Local Church will have discipline when necessary.)*
Assuredly, I say to you, whatever you bind on earth will be bound in heaven, and whatever you loose on earth will be loosed in heaven. *(God's authority will be channeled through the Local Church.)*

Again I say to you, that if two *(One person cannot make up a Local Church.)*
of you agree on earth concerning anything that they ask, it will be done for them by My Father in heaven. *(The Local Church will function in unity and agreement.)*
For where two or three *(The Church is not a building, but people.)*
are gathered together in My name, *(The Local Church will be a gathering of believers identified with the name of Jesus Christ.)*
I am there in the midst of them." *(The Lord will dwell in the midst of the Local Church.)*

I believe that in the following Scriptures Jesus is talking about the role of the Church after His death, resurrection and ascension. (If not the future Church, who could it be?)

Matthew 18:2–4 Then Jesus called a little child to Him, set him in the midst of them, and said, "Assuredly, I say to you, unless you are converted and become as little children, you will by no means enter the kingdom of heaven. Therefore whoever humbles himself as this little child is the greatest in the kingdom of heaven." *(The Church will walk in humility.)*

Matthew 24:14 "And this gospel of the kingdom will be preached in all the world as a witness to all the nations, and then the end will come." *(The Church will preach the "Gospel of the Kingdom" to all nations.)*

And if that is true, then the "THE GREAT COMMISSION" is also to the Church in the Book of Acts and beyond.

Looking in Matthew 28:18–20 And Jesus came and spoke to them, saying, "All authority has been given to Me in heaven and on earth. Go therefore and make disciples of all the nations, *(The Church will go to all nations and make disciples)*
baptizing them in the name of the Father and of the Son and of the Holy Spirit, *(The Church will baptize believers.)*
teaching *(The Church will teach the Word of God.)*

them to observe (Strong's: 5083 - to attend to carefully) all things that I have commanded you; *(Members of the Church will be doers not just hearers.)*
and lo, I am with you always, even to the end of the age." Amen. *(The Church is never alone.)*

Mark 16:15–18 And He said to them, "Go into all the world and preach the gospel to every creature. He who believes and is baptized will be saved; *(The Church will baptize believers.)*
but he who does not believe will be condemned. And these signs will follow those who believe: In My name they will cast out demons; *(The Church will cast out demons.)*
they will speak with new tongues; *(Members of the Church will speak in new tongues.)*
they will take up serpents; and if they drink anything deadly, it will by no means hurt them; *(I do not feel qualified to address these thoughts.)*
they will lay hands on the sick, and they will recover." *(The Church will pray for the sick.)*

Luke 24:47–49 and that repentance and remission of sins should be preached in His name to all nations, beginning at Jerusalem. And you are witnesses of these things. "Behold, I send the Promise of My Father upon you; but tarry in the city of Jerusalem until you are endued with power *(The Church will be endued with power.)* from on high." *(That power is supernatural power from God.)*

And I believe that in John 21:15–19, Jesus, in talking to Peter about his future, is also speaking to the future church.

John 21:15–19 So when they had eaten breakfast, Jesus said to Simon Peter, "Simon, son of Jonah, do you love Me more than these?" *(Believers will love Jesus more than anything else.)*
He said to Him, "Yes, Lord; You know that I love You." He said to him, feed My lambs." *(The leaders of the Church will feed, with the "Bread of Life" both those young in the Lord as well as those young in years.)*
He said to him again a second time, "Simon, son of Jonah, do you love Me?" He said to Him, "Yes, Lord; You know that I love You."

He said to him, "Tend (Strong's: 4165 KJV translates as "shepherd" 15 times, "Shepherd" twice, and "pastor" once.) *(The leaders of the Church will not only feed the flock but also tend them as a shepherd tends his sheep.)*
My sheep." *(Each member of God's Church belongs to Jesus!)*
He said to him the third time, "Simon, son of Jonah, do you love Me?" Peter was grieved because He said to him the third time, "Do you love Me?" And he said to Him, "Lord, You know all things; You know that I love You." Jesus said to him, "Feed My sheep. Most assuredly, I say to you, when you were younger, you girded yourself and walked where you wished; but when you are old, you will stretch out your hands, and another will gird you and carry you where you do not wish." *(Those in the Church will not live unto themselves but unto Jesus.)*
This He spoke, signifying by what death he would glorify God. And when He had spoken this, He said to him, "Follow Me." *(The Church will follow Jesus in all things.)*

Other thoughts Jesus shared that I believe address the Church in the Book of Acts and beyond:

Matthew 4:19 Then He said to them, "Follow Me, and I will make you fishers of men." *(The Church will be evangelistic.)*

Matthew 6:33 (KJV) "But seek ye first the kingdom of God, and his righteousness; and all these things shall be added unto you." *(The Church will put God first.)*

Matthew 10:28 (KJV) "And fear not them which kill the body, but are not able to kill the soul: but rather fear him which is able to destroy both soul and body in hell." *(The Church will fear God and not be afraid of satan.)*

Matthew 15:4 "For God commanded, saying, 'Honor your father and your mother'; and, 'He who curses father or mother, let him be put to death.'" *(The Church honors those who nurtured it both in the natural and in the Spirit.)*

Matthew 26:26-28 And as they were eating, Jesus took bread, blessed and broke it, and gave it to the disciples and said, "Take, eat; this is My body." Then He took the cup, and gave thanks, and gave it to them, saying, "Drink from it, all of you. For this is My blood of the new covenant, which is shed for many for the remission of sins." *(The Church will acknowledge and celebrate Jesus' death, burial and resurrection by taking communion.)*

Luke 9:23–24 Then He said to them all, "If anyone desires to come after Me, let him deny himself, and take up his cross daily, and follow Me. For whoever desires to save his life will lose it, but whoever loses his life for My sake will save it. *(Individual members of the Church will deny themselves for Christ's sake.)*

John 3:3-6 Jesus answered and said to him, "Most assuredly, I say to you, unless one is born again, he cannot see the kingdom of God." ... Jesus answered, "Most assuredly, I say to you, unless one is born of water and the Spirit, he cannot enter the kingdom of God. That which is born of the flesh is flesh, and that which is born of the Spirit is spirit. Do not marvel that I said to you, 'You must be born again.'" *(Humanity will enter the Church by new birth.)*

John 7:38-39 "He who believes in Me, as the Scripture has said, out of his heart will flow rivers of living water." But this He spoke concerning the Spirit, whom those believing in Him would receive; for the Holy Spirit was not yet given, because Jesus was not yet glorified. *(God's Church will have such an abundance of His presence that it will flow out like a river.)*

John 13:34 "A new commandment I give to you, that you love one another; as I have loved you, that you also love one another." *(God's children will love one another with God's kind of love.)*

John 14:12 "Most assuredly, I say to you, he who believes in Me, the works that I do he will do also; and greater works than these he will do, because I go to My Father." *(The Church will do the works that Jesus did and even greater works.)*

John 14:19-23 (NIV) "Before long, the world will not see me anymore, but you will see me. Because I live, you also will live. On that day you will realize that I am in my Father, and you are in me, and I am in you. Whoever has my commands and obeys them, he is the one who loves me. He who loves me will be loved by my Father, and I too will love him and show myself to him." ... Jesus replied, "If anyone loves me, he will obey my teaching. My Father will love him, and we will come to him and make our home with him." *(God will live in the hearts of individuals in His Church.)*

John 15:9 "As the Father loved Me, I also have loved you; abide in My love." *(The Church will live in the love of God.)*

John 16:33 "These things I have spoken to you, that in Me you may have peace. *(The Church will have peace in Christ.)*
In the world you will have tribulation; but be of good cheer, I have overcome the world." *(In the world, the Church will have tests and trials.)*

John 17:20 "I do not pray for these alone, but also for those who will believe in Me through their word; that they all may be one, as You, Father, are in Me, and I in You; that they also may be one in Us, that the world may believe that You sent Me." *(The Church will be one with God and one with one another.)*

As we contemplate the words of Jesus concerning the future Church, we get some insight into what that future Church is supposed to be like. This is not a picture of the way we are supposed to <u>do</u> Church as much as it is a picture of what the Church <u>is</u> in its nature and character.

But it doesn't stop here, we also get to look at the recorded history of how the Church developed and see how some of these actual traits, and more, get built into the newly-birthed Church. We have it written down for us in that wonderful book in the Bible we call The Acts of the Apostles.

DISCUSSION QUESTIONS FOR CHAPTER 2

Why do you think it is important that we begin with the words of Jesus?

Had you already noticed that Jesus talked so much about the future Church?

Did you find any traits that should be a part of the Church that were new to you?

If so, what were they and how can you implement them into your life?

Have you seen some traits in the words of Jesus that I missed?

Can you think of any examples of the things Jesus taught that you have already seen happen in the Church?

TRAITS OF THE DEVELOPING CHURCH AS FOUND IN THE BOOK OF ACTS

In the book of Acts, we find these traits of the Church, some universal and some local, as they are experienced by a living and growing Church. This is the Church, being led by the Holy Spirit, as it goes about discovering what it means to be the Church, something that had never been on earth before.

We will use the same pattern that we used with the words of Jesus to unveil these traits from Scripture passages in Acts:

Acts 1:4–8 And being assembled together with them, He commanded them not to depart from Jerusalem, but to wait for the Promise of the Father, "which," He said, "you have heard from Me; for John truly baptized with water, but you shall be baptized with the Holy Spirit not many days from now." *(Believers are baptized with the Holy Spirit.)*
Therefore, when they had come together, they asked Him, saying, "Lord, will You at this time restore the kingdom to Israel?" And He said to them, "It is not for you to know times or seasons which the Father has put in His own authority. But you shall receive power when the Holy Spirit has come upon you; *(The baptism of the Holy Spirit brings "power from on high" to each believer.)*
and you shall be witnesses (Strong's: 3144 [martus]; AV translates as "witness" 29 times, "martyr" three times, and "record" twice.)

(Believers are to be witnesses (possibly even martyrs) to the ends of the earth.)
to Me in Jerusalem, and in all Judea and Samaria, and to the end of the earth." *(The Gospel is for the whole world.)*

Acts 1:14 These all continued with one accord in prayer and supplication, with the women and Mary the mother of Jesus, and with His brothers." *(The Church prays in unity.)*

Acts 2:1–4 When the Day of Pentecost had fully come, they were all with one accord in one place. And suddenly there came a sound from heaven, as of a rushing mighty wind, and it filled the whole house where they were sitting. Then there appeared to them divided tongues, as of fire, and one sat upon each of them. And they were all filled with the Holy Spirit and began to speak with other tongues, as the Spirit gave them utterance. *(The Church has access to the Supernatural.)*

Acts 2:14 But Peter, standing up with the eleven, raised his voice and said to them, "Men of Judea and all who dwell in Jerusalem, let this be known to you, and heed my words." (See also Acts 2:37–38) *(The Church is not hesitant to preach the Gospel.)*

Acts 2:42 And they continued steadfastly in the apostles' doctrine and fellowship, in the breaking of bread, and in prayers. *(The Church gathers for teaching, fellowship, food and prayer.)*

Acts 2:44–47 Now all who believed were together, and had all things in common, and sold their possessions and goods, and divided them among all, as anyone had need. *(Believers take care of each other.)*
So continuing daily with one accord in the temple, *(The Church gathers in large groups.)*
and breaking bread from house to house, *(The Local Church gathers in small groups.)*
they ate their food with gladness and simplicity of heart, *(The Church has fellowship together.)*
praising God and having favor with all the people. And the Lord added to the church daily *(The Church is added to by Jesus Christ*

Himself.)
those who were being saved. *(All are welcome to come but only the saved are added to the Church.)*

Acts 3:6–8 Then Peter said, "Silver and gold I do not have, but what I do have I give you: In the name of Jesus Christ of Nazareth, rise up and walk." And he took him by the right hand and lifted him up, and immediately his feet and ankle bones received strength. So he, leaping up, stood and walked and entered the temple with them—walking, leaping, and praising God. (See also Acts 5:15) *(The Church performs miracles and signs and wonders outside their walls.)*

Acts 4:10 "let it be known to you all, and to all the people of Israel, that by the name of Jesus Christ of Nazareth, whom you crucified, whom God raised from the dead, by Him this man stands here before you whole." *(The message of the Church is Jesus Christ crucified, raised from the dead and living in His Church.)*

Acts 4:12 "Nor is there salvation in any other, for there is no other name under heaven given among men by which we must be saved." (See also Acts 8:4) *(The Church boldly proclaims the need _for_ and the only way _of_ salvation.)*

Acts 5:4–5a "While it remained, was it not your own? And after it was sold, was it not in your own control? Why have you conceived this thing in your heart? You have not lied to men but to God." Then Ananias, hearing these words, fell down and breathed his last. *(Church members are honest and people of integrity.)*

Acts 5:5 Then Ananias, hearing these words, fell down and breathed his last. So great fear came upon all those who heard these things. *(The Church is disciplined by Christ Himself.)*

Acts 5:13-14 Yet none of the rest dared join them, but the people esteemed them highly. *(People don't join the Church in an intellectual way; God adds them as family through new birth.)*

And believers were increasingly added to the Lord, multitudes of both men and women. *(The Church is an assembly of believers in Christ, part of Christ Himself.)*

Acts 6:3–4 "Therefore, brethren, seek out from among you seven men of good reputation, full of the Holy Spirit and wisdom, whom we may appoint over this business; *(The Church cares for one another.)*
but we will give ourselves continually to prayer and to the ministry of the word." (See also Acts 11:26, Acts 12:5 and Acts 13:3) *(The Church prays and teaches the Word.)*

Acts 7:59–60 And they stoned Stephen as he was calling on God and saying, "Lord Jesus, receive my spirit." Then he knelt down and cried out with a loud voice, "Lord, do not charge them with this sin." And when he had said this, he fell asleep. *(The Church is bold to preach and quick to forgive.)*

Acts 8:1 ... At that time a great persecution arose against the church which was at Jerusalem.... *(The Church is a congregation or assembly of people active in a given locality.)*

Acts 8:7 For unclean spirits, crying with a loud voice, came out of many who were possessed; and many who were paralyzed and lame were healed. *(Demon-possessed people are set free through the Church.)*

Acts 8:37-38 Then Philip said, "If you believe with all your heart, you may (be baptized)." And he answered and said, "I believe that Jesus Christ is the Son of God." So he commanded the chariot to stand still. And both Philip and the eunuch went down into the water, and he baptized him. *(Believers are to be baptized in water.)*

Acts 9:20–21 Immediately he (Paul) preached the Christ in the synagogues, that He is the Son of God. Then all who heard were amazed, and said, "Is this not he who destroyed those who called on this name in Jerusalem, and has come here for that purpose, so that he might bring them bound to the chief priests?" *(The Church gives second chances.)*

Acts 10:34–35 Then Peter opened his mouth and said: "In truth I perceive that God shows no partiality. But in every nation whoever fears Him and works righteousness is accepted by Him." *(The Church includes people from every race.)*

Acts 11:27 And in these days prophets came from Jerusalem to Antioch. Then one of them, named Agabus, stood up and showed by the Spirit that there was going to be a great famine throughout all the world, which also happened in the days of Claudius Caesar. *(The Church is prophetic.)*

Acts 13:1-3 Now in the church that was at Antioch there were certain prophets and teachers: Barnabas, Simeon who was called Niger, Lucius of Cyrene, Manaen who had been brought up with Herod the tetrarch, and Saul. *(The Church has various kinds of ministry.)*
they ministered to the Lord and fasted, the Holy Spirit said, *(The Holy Spirit has preeminence in the Church.)*
"Now separate to Me Barnabas and Saul for the work to which I have called them. *(The Local Church operates using team ministry.)*
...they sent them away." *(The Church sends ministry to diverse places.)*
Then, having fasted and prayed, *(The Church fasts and prays.)*
and laid hands on them... *(The Church practices the laying on of hands.)*

Acts 14:15 "...Men, why are you doing these things? We also are men with the same nature as you, and preach to you that you should turn from these useless things to the living God, who made the heaven, the earth, the sea, and all things that are in them." *(The Church is made up of ordinary people not super saints.)*

Acts 14:23 So when they had appointed elders in every church, and prayed with fasting, they commended them to the Lord in whom they had believed." *(The Church fasts and prays.)*

Acts 15:3-4 So, being sent on their way by the church .... And when they had come to Jerusalem, they were received by the church and the apostles and the elders; and they reported all things that God had done with them. *(The Church is joined in voluntary fellowship with other local churches.)*

Acts 15:22 Then it pleased the apostles and elders, with the whole church, to send chosen men of their own company to Antioch with Paul and Barnabas, namely, Judas who was also named Barsabas, and Silas, leading men among the brethren. *(Each Local Church is a complete unit in itself with corporate authority.)*

Acts 15:29 "that you abstain from things offered to idols, *(The Church refrains from contact with idols.)*
from blood, from things strangled, and from sexual immorality. If you keep yourselves from these, you will do well." *(The Church refrains from sexual immorality.)*

Acts 15:39 Then the contention became so sharp that they parted from one another. And so Barnabas took Mark and sailed to Cyprus. *(The Church is not perfect.)*

Acts 16:4-5 And as they went through the cities, they delivered to them the decrees to keep, which were determined by the apostles and elders at Jerusalem. *(The Local Church learns from other Local Churches.)*
So the churches were strengthened in the faith, and increased in number daily. *(The Church is a place established in the faith (doctrine).)*

Acts 16:25 But at midnight Paul and Silas were praying and singing hymns to God, and the prisoners were listening to them. *(Singing is a part of Church worship.)*

Acts 20:27-28 "For I have not shunned to declare to you the whole counsel of God. *(The Church teaches the whole Bible.)*

Therefore take heed to yourselves and to all the flock, among which the Holy Spirit has made you overseers, to shepherd the church of God which He purchased with His own blood." *(The Church has individuals ordained in positions of authority to exercise leadership, discipline and oversight.)*

You might not agree with all the traits that I have listed above. You might want to remove some of them or you might feel that I missed some. I am just showing you what I found after my eyes were opened to God's pattern for the Church that He had hidden in His Word.

I believe that all of these traits are confirmed and expanded upon in the rest of the New Testament books. For example, Jesus giving to the Church what they need.

Ephesians 4:8, 11–16 Therefore He says: "When He ascended on high, He led captivity captive, And gave gifts to men." ...And He Himself gave some to be apostles, some prophets, some evangelists, and some pastors and teachers, for the equipping of the saints for the work of ministry, for the edifying of the body of Christ, till we all come to the unity of the faith and of the knowledge of the Son of God, to a perfect man, to the measure of the stature of the fullness of Christ; that we should no longer be children, tossed to and fro and carried about with every wind of doctrine, by the trickery of men, in the cunning craftiness of deceitful plotting, but, speaking the truth in love, may grow up in all things into Him who is the head—Christ—from whom the whole body, joined and knit together by what every joint supplies, according to the effective working by which every part does its share, causes growth of the body for the edifying of itself in love.

Interestingly enough, Jesus gave these gifts for a purpose. The apostle Paul states, "Therefore, King Agrippa, I was not disobedient to the heavenly vision." (Acts 26:19) God has a vision for where the Church is to go. May I be so bold as to say that His purpose has not yet been completed, that it is the responsibility of the above mentioned ministry to aim the Church at the goals of

Ephesians 11-16 and that we are not fulfilling our calling if we only declare the part of the Gospel that deals with salvation?

DISCUSSION QUESTIONS FOR CHAPTER 3

What are some traits from the book of Acts that help define the Church that are new to you?

Have you seen some traits in the book of Acts that I missed?

What are you doing now or can do in the future to help the fulfillment of that vision for Jesus' Church to be a glorious Church equipped for ministry and displaying Christ-likeness?

THE TRAITS

As you read through the traits found in the Gospels and the Book of Acts, I'm sure you noticed that some of these traits apply to the Universal Church, some to the Local Church, and some to the individual believers in the Church. I have found it hard to make those distinctions in a consistent manner. To me, the Universal Church is made up of Local Churches which are made up of individual believers. Every trait applies to all of them, the Universal Church is the macrocosm and the individual believer is the microcosm. To a certain extent each reflects the other; you can't have one without the other. I believe that as you look through them again in the following list, you will see ways that the interaction, the by-play of Universal application of a trait, works with the Local application of the trait, and the individual application of the trait. There are some that fit in just one, eg. the Church is a family. It is hard for one person to call himself a family. Likewise, it is hard to think of the Universal Church being baptized, individual believers are baptized. Think about this as you go through the following simplified list of traits.

1. The Church loves God; Father, Son and Holy Spirit.
2. The Church is not a building but people.
3. The Church is built on revelation from God.
4. The Church has a firm foundation.
5. God, through Jesus Christ, commissioned the Church.
6. Jesus Christ is building the Church.
7. The Church belongs to Jesus.

8.   Satan is the enemy of the Church.

9.   Through Jesus Christ, the Church is victorious.

10.   Jesus gives the Church what it needs.

11.   The Church is a Spiritual entity.

12.   The Church has purpose.

13.   The Church represents the authority of Christ on earth.

14.   God's authority is channeled through the Local Church.

15.   God hears and responds to the Church.

16.   The Church is living, not stagnant.

17.   The Local Church is a spiritual family.

18.   The Church is not perfect.

19.   Until the Church is perfect, there will be a great need for love, patience and forgiveness.

20.   The Local Church is active.

21.   The Local Church has order.

22.   One person cannot make up a Local Church.

23.   The Local Church exercises unity and agreement.

24.   Jesus dwells in the midst of the Church.

25.   The Church goes to all nations and makes disciples.

26.   Believers are witnesses (possibly even martyrs) to the ends of the earth.

27.   The Local Church baptizes believers in water.

28.   The Church teaches the entire Word of God.

29.   The Church is made up of doers, not just hearers.

30.   Members of the Church speak in new tongues.

31.   The Church prays for the sick.

32.   Through the Holy Spirit, the Church is endued with supernatural power from God.

33.   The Church loves Jesus more than anything else.

34.   The leaders of the Church feed, with the "Bread of Life," both those young in the Lord as well as those young in years.

35.   The leaders of the Local Church not only feed the flock but also tend them as a shepherd tends his sheep.

36.   Those in the Church do not live unto themselves but unto God.

37.   The Church follows Jesus.

38.   The Church is evangelistic.

39.   The Church puts God first.

40.   The Church fears God, not satan.

41. The Church honors those who nurture it both in the natural and in the Spirit.
42. The Church walks in humility.
43. The Church lives in the love of God.
44. The Church acknowledges and celebrates Jesus' death, burial and resurrection by taking communion.
45. God's Church has such an abundance of His presence that it flows out like a river.
46. The Church does the same works that Jesus did and even greater works.
47. God will live in the hearts of individuals in His Church.
48. In the midst of trials and tribulation the Church has peace.
49. The Church is one with God and one with one another.
50. Believers are baptized with the Holy Spirit.
51. The baptism of the Holy Spirit brings "power from on high" to each believer.
52. The Church lives in the supernatural.
53. The Church preaches the Good News of Jesus Christ.
54. The Church gathers for teaching, fellowship, food and prayer.
55. Believers love and take care of each other.
56. The Local Church gathers both in large groups and in small groups.
57. All are welcome to gather together with the Church, but only the saved are added to the Church.
58. The Local Church takes miracles and signs and wonders into their city.
59. The message of the Church is Jesus Christ crucified, raised from the dead and living in His Church.
60. The Church boldly proclaims the need for and the way of salvation.
61. Church members are people of honesty and integrity.
62. The Church is disciplined by Christ Himself.
63. People don't join the Church, God adds them.
64. The Local Church is an assembly of believers in Christ, part of Christ Himself.
65. Miracles of healing are worked in the name of Jesus by the Church.
66. The Church leaders pray and preach the Word.

67. The Church is bold to preach and quick to forgive.
68. The Local Church is a congregation or assembly of people in a given locality.
69. The Church carries the Word everywhere they go.
70. Demon-possessed people are set free through the Church.
71. The Church believes in second chances.
72. The Church includes people from every race.
73. The Church has various kinds of ministry.
74 The Church is prophetic.
75. The Holy Spirit moves and has authority in the Church.
76. Ministry is sent out from the Local Church.
77. The Local Church operates using team ministry.
78. The Church fasts and prays.
79. The Church practices the laying on of hands.
80. The Local Church has individuals ordained in positions of authority to exercise leadership, discipline and oversight.
81. The Church is made up of ordinary people not super- saints.
82. Local Churches join in voluntary fellowship with other Local Churches.
83. Each Local Church is a complete unit in itself with corporate authority.
84. The Church refrains from contact with idols.
85. The Church refrains from sexual immorality.
86. The Local Church learns from other Local Churches.
87. The Church is established in the faith (doctrine).

GROUPING THE TRAITS

As I pondered these traits, I started thinking of ways to group the traits so they would be easier to understand. About that time, I was visiting my daughter, Susan Perkins, whose doctoral studies included training in qualitative research. (She had worked with large data sets when she wrote her doctoral thesis.) She read the list and said, "Dad, this is easy. I can already see how they can be grouped in a very natural way." The following (with a little input from me) is her grouping put into a graphic representation.

> *God pours of Himself into His Church so that the Church can pour into the world.*

In the graph below, please notice the following: God surrounds and touches everything including the world, and the Church is in the world but not of the world.

At the top, God directly impacts the Church by nature, by Jesus, by His Word, by the Holy Spirit, and etc. God pours of Himself into His Church so that the Church can pour into the world.

At the bottom, the Church impacts the world through actions. Some of these actions are spiritual; mission work, preaching the Gospel, praying for the sick, praying against principalities and powers in heavenly places, and more. Some of these actions are natural; building church buildings, building schools, building hospitals, helping the poor, taking medical help to other nations, helping areas that have gone through natural disasters, and etc. All of these actions are practical and impact the world around us.

As God established the Church, He first of all set the stage for the Church. In setting the stage, the Church's spiritual foundation (apostles and prophets, Jesus the chief cornerstone - see Ephesians 2:20) was established along with practical distinctions that show the character and nature of the Church.

At the heart of the church are believers who have their own personal relationships with Christ thus the relationship between

God and His Church is a result of individual relationships. I put this at the heart because relationship defines who we are in Christ and influences every other aspect of what the Church is and does.

Then we see God defining the Church in a more specific way. This includes its organization and structure; apostles, prophets, evangelists, pastors, teachers, bishops, elders, various ministries and giftings, and etc. Along with the organizational aspects of the Church, God also gives different descriptions of a well-working Church; humble, loving, prophetic, and etc.

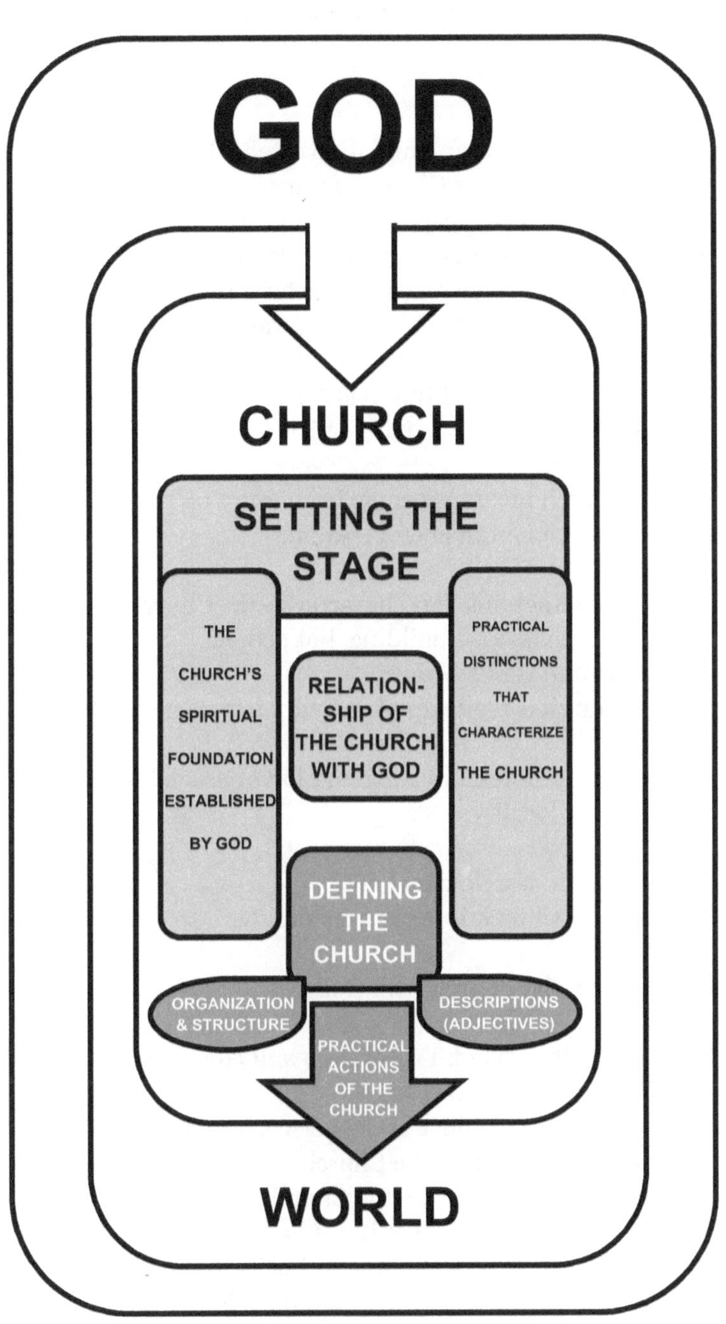

GOD
CHURCH
SETTING THE STAGE
THE CHURCH'S SPIRITUAL FOUNDATION ESTABLISHED BY GOD
RELATION-SHIP OF THE CHURCH WITH GOD
PRACTICAL DISTINCTIONS THAT CHARACTERIZE THE CHURCH
DEFINING THE CHURCH
ORGANIZATION & STRUCTURE
DESCRIPTIONS (ADJECTIVES)
PRACTICAL ACTIONS OF THE CHURCH
WORLD

TRAITS OF THE CHURCH

I. Setting the stage

    A. The Church's Spiritual foundation established by God
        1. God, through Jesus Christ, commissioned the Church.
        2. The Church has a firm foundation.
        3. The Church is built on revelation from God.
        4. The Church is established in the faith (doctrine).
        5. The Church lives in the supernatural.
        6. The Church has purpose.
        7. The message of the Church is Jesus Christ crucified, raised from the dead, living in His Church and coming again.
        8. The Church includes people from every race.
        9. The Church has an enemy—satan.

    B. Practical distinctions that characterize the Church
        1. The Church is not a building, but people.
        2. The Church is not perfect.
        3. The Church is made up of ordinary people not super-saints.
        4. The Local Church is a congregation or assembly of people in a given locality.
        5. The Church is living, not stagnant.
        6. The Church is a Spiritual entity.
        7. The Local Church is a Spiritual family.

II. Relationship of the Church with God

    A. The Church loves God; Father, Son and Holy Spirit.
    B. The Church belongs to Jesus.
    C. Jesus dwells in the midst of the Local Church.
    D. Jesus Christ is building the Church.
    E. God hears and responds to the Church.
    F. Jesus gives the Church what it needs.
    G. The Holy Spirit moves and has authority in the Church.
    H. God will live in the hearts of individuals in His Church.

I. Through the Holy Spirit, the Church is endued with supernatural power from God.

J. The Church represents the authority of Christ on earth.

K. God's authority is channeled through the Local Church.

L. God's Church has such an abundance of His presence that it flows out like a river.

M. The Church is disciplined by Christ Himself.

III. Defining the Church

A. Organization and working structure of the Church
   1. One person cannot make up a Local Church.
   2. The Local Church is an assembly of believers in Christ, part of Christ Himself.
   3. The Church gathers both in large groups and in small groups.
   4. People don't join the Church, God adds them.
   5. All are welcome to gather together with the Church, but only the saved are added to the Church.
   6. The Local Church has individuals ordained in positions of authority to exercise leadership, discipline and oversight.
   7. The Local Church has order.
   8. Each Local Church is a complete unit in itself with corporate authority.
   9. The Church operates using team ministry.
   10. The Church leaders pray and preach the Word.
   11. The leaders of the Local Church tend the flock as a shepherd tends his sheep.
   12. The leaders of the Church feed, with the "Bread of Life," both those young in the Lord as well as those young in years.
   13. Local Churches join in voluntary fellowship with other Local Churches
   14. The Local Church learns from other Local Churches.
   15. Ministry is sent out from the Church.

B. Descriptions of a well-working Church
   1. The Local Church is active.
   2. Believers are witnesses (possibly even martyrs) to the

ends of the earth.
3. Through Jesus Christ the Church is victorious.
4. The Church is one with God and one with one another.
5. The Local Church exercises unity and agreement.
6. The Church honors those who nurtured it both in the natural and in the Spirit.
7. Those in the Church do not live unto themselves but unto God.
8. The Church lives in the love of God.
9. The Church walks in humility.
10. Church members are people of honesty and integrity.
11. In the midst of trials and tribulation the Church has peace.
12. The Church has various kinds of ministry.
13. The Church is prophetic.
14. The Church refrains from sexual immorality.
15. The Church refrains from contact with idols.
16. Demon-possessed people are set free through the Church.
17. The Church believes in second chances.
18. Until the Church is perfect, there will be a great need for love, patience and forgiveness.

C. Practical actions of the Church
1. The Church loves Jesus more than anything else.
2. The Church acknowledges and celebrates Jesus' death, burial and resurrection by taking communion.
3. The Church follows Jesus.
4. The Church puts God first.
5. The Church fears God, not satan.
6. The Church is evangelistic.
7. The Church baptizes believers in water.
8. The Church teaches the entire Word of God.
9. The Church fasts and prays.
10. The Church gathers for teaching, fellowship, food and prayer.
11. The Church prays for the sick.
12. Miracles of healing are worked in the name of Jesus by the Church.

13. The Church takes miracles and signs and wonders outside its walls.
14. The Church is made up of doers, not just hearers.
15. The Church goes to all nations and makes disciples.
16. The Church carries the Word everywhere they go.
17. Believers are baptized with the Holy Spirit.
18. Members of the Church speak in new tongues.
19. The baptism of the Holy Spirit brings "power from on high" to each believer.
20. The Church practices the laying on of hands.
21. The Church does the works that Jesus did and even greater works.
22. The Church boldly proclaims the need for and the way of salvation.
23. The Church preaches the Good News of Jesus Christ.
24. The Church is bold to preach and quick to forgive.
25. Believers love and take care of each other.

If you were the one grouping these traits, what groups would you put them in?

What is your reasoning behind these groups?

Draw a diagram using your groupings.

Describe the meaning of your diagram.

What traits do you already see in your church and what traits do you hope to see?

How can you help in the development of these traits?

PART II

INSIGHT ON THE CHURCH
FROM THE OLD TESTAMENT

INSIGHT ON THE CHURCH
FROM THE OLD TESTAMENT

We get a lot of insight into lessons the New Testament Church is supposed to learn from the Old Testament through the writings of the Apostle Paul. His letters tell us that he was a Pharisee trained by Gamaliel and by the time he was an adult, he was a very learned scholar.

The online Encyclopedia Britannica says this about Paul. *"Until about the midpoint of his life, Paul was a member of the Pharisees, a religious party that emerged during the later Second Temple period. What little is known about Paul the Pharisee reflects the character of the Pharisaic movement. Pharisees believed in life after death, which was one of Paul's deepest convictions. They accepted nonbiblical traditions as being about as important as the written Bible; Paul refers to his expertise in traditions. (Galatians 1:14) Pharisees were very careful students of the Hebrew Bible, and Paul was able to quote extensively from the Greek translation."*

In his letters, the Apostle Paul quotes at least 268 verses from the Old Testament. In 1 Corinthians 10:1-11, the Apostle Paul wrote a lot about the New Testament Church learning from what happened to Israel in the Old Testament. If you are not familiar with that portion of Scripture you might take the time to read it now. In 1 Corinthians 10:6 Paul writes, "Now these things (verses 1-5) became our examples, to the intent that we should not lust after evil things as they also lusted." And then again, still speaking about Israel's actions in the Old Testament (verses 7-10), Paul writes in 1 Corinthians 10:11, "Now all these things happened to them as examples, and they were written for our admonition, upon whom the ends of the ages have come." The Merriam-Webster Dictionary (1996) defines admonition as a "gentle or friendly reproof, counsel or warning against fault or oversight." So, according to the Apostle Paul, we can learn from the examples in the Old Testament how to be better Christians in the New Testament.

In Part 2 we will be looking at a specific time-frame in Old Testament history; the time of Israel's journey from Egypt to Canaan's land and the building of the Tabernacle of Moses.

THE CHURCH IN THE WILDERNESS

As mentioned in my introduction, just before he was stoned, Stephen, speaking of Moses, made this statement: "This is he, that was in <u>the church in the wilderness</u>...." (Acts 7:38 KJV) Stephen didn't say the Church in the Promised Land, or the Church under the kings, or the church in Babylon, he said "the church in the wilderness." Why did the Holy Spirit prompt Stephen to say it just that way? I believe it was because there are important parallels between the Israelites as they traveled to the Promised Land and the newly saved Christian as he or she progresses in his or her new life in Christ. In this chapter, I list several aspects of what the Israelites faced as they traveled to the Promised Land and explore how they apply to the journey of a new Christian.

- **The Israelites, the church in the wilderness, were leaving their captivity in Egypt and going to a land flowing with milk and honey, promised to them by God Himself.**

The new Christian is leaving the world of sin and bondage and going to the place Jesus promised when He said: "In My Father's house are many mansions; if it were not so, I would

> *Anything that holds us back or drags us down must be left behind.*

have told you. I go to prepare a place for you. And if I go and prepare a place for you, I will come again and receive you to

Myself; that where I am, there you may be also." (John 14:2–3) The parallel here is that when we are born again we are supposed to leave our old life behind us. We are not to carry that old life along with us on the way to our future home. The Scriptures tell us "… if anyone is in Christ, he is a new creation; old things have passed away; behold, all things have become new." (2 Corinthians 5:17)

At times along the way, Israel didn't want to let go of the past. They longed for the leeks, garlic and security of Egypt. Even though they had been mistreated in their former home by their slave masters, they weren't always happy with their new leader, Moses. So, likewise, new believers want to hold on to things from their past life that appear to be good but must instead "… lay aside every weight, and the sin which so easily ensnares us, and let us run with endurance the race that is set before us." (Hebrews 12:1) Everything from our past life is not wrong but we have to recognize that along with sin there are also weights, things that hold us back, distractions that keep us from being focused on the new creation we are in Christ. These things, like the leaks and garlic, might not be evil but anything that holds us back or drags us down must be left behind.

- **The Israelites, the church in the wilderness, were going to have to learn about the God who delivered them from Egypt.**

For over 400 years Israel had lived among a people who worshipped idols. During those many years, they would have picked up an understanding of those gods even if they didn't worship them. And some of the Israelites worshipped the false gods of Egypt and even carried idols to these false gods as they traveled through the wilderness. Amos 5:25–26 tells us that. "Did you offer Me sacrifices and offerings In the wilderness forty years, O house of Israel? You also carried Sikkuth your king and Chiun, your idols, the star of your gods, which you made for yourselves." Egypt had many gods so Israel might have thought it was acceptable to continue worshiping the gods of Egypt and just add "I AM" into the mix. To fix that, God gave the Israelites the Ten Commandments and all the Law through Moses. Before Moses passed God's laws on to the Israelites they really had no clue about this "I AM", the God of their fathers.

Brand new babies in Christ, like the Israelites, don't have much of an understanding of God. In fact, many of the things new believers think they know about God are wrong. The world's information about God has been gleaned from movies, cartoons, conversations with people who are not even believers but think that they know what Christians believe; everywhere but the Bible. This, then, becomes an important role of the Church: to teach, with the help of the Holy Spirit, the whole counsel of God; to unfold the truth of who God really is and to help believers understand not just the works of God but also His ways. I believe a good illustration of this is found in Paul's exhortation to the Church in Ephesus.

Ephesians 4:20–5:11 "But you have not so learned Christ, if indeed you have heard Him and have been taught by Him, as the truth is in Jesus: that you put off, concerning your former conduct, the old man which grows corrupt according to the deceitful lusts, and be renewed in the spirit of your mind, and that you put on the new man which was created according to God, in true righteousness and holiness. Therefore, putting away lying, 'Let each one of you speak truth with his neighbor,' for we are members of one another. 'Be angry, and do not sin': do not let the sun go down on your wrath, nor give place to the devil. Let him who stole steal no longer, but rather let him labor, working with his hands what is good, that he may have something to give him who has need. Let no corrupt word proceed out of your mouth, but what is good for necessary edification, that it may impart grace to the hearers. And do not grieve the Holy Spirit of God, by whom you were sealed for the day of redemption. Let all bitterness, wrath, anger, clamor, and evil speaking be put away from you, with all malice. And be kind to one another, tenderhearted, forgiving one another, even as God in Christ forgave you. Therefore be imitators of God as dear children. And walk in love, as Christ also has loved us and given Himself for us, an offering and a sacrifice to God for a sweet-smelling aroma. But fornication and all uncleanness or covetousness, let it not even be named among you, as is fitting for saints; neither filthiness, nor foolish talking, nor coarse jesting, which are not fitting, but rather giving of thanks. For this you know, that no fornicator, unclean person, nor covetous man, who is an idolater, has any inheritance in the kingdom of Christ and God. Let no one deceive you with empty words, for because of these things the wrath of God comes upon the sons of disobedience. Therefore do not be partakers with them. For you were once darkness, but now you are light in the Lord. Walk as children of light (for the fruit of the Spirit is in all goodness, righteousness, and truth), finding out what is acceptable to the Lord. And have no fellowship with the unfruitful works of darkness, but rather expose them."

- **The Israelites, the church in the wilderness, were given supernatural provision along their way.**

As they traveled through the wilderness, God provided Israel with everything they needed.

The Church is also given supernatural provision on their journey. The Israelites were given water from the rock, "...For they drank of that spiritual Rock that followed them, and that Rock was Christ." (1 Corinthians 10:4) Jesus was the Spiritual Rock that followed Israel in the wilderness and provided water. John 4:14 "but whoever drinks of the water that I shall give him will never thirst. But the water that I shall give him will become in him a fountain of water springing up into everlasting life."

The Israelites were also given manna (bread) to eat. Heavenly bread: John 6:48–51, "I (Jesus) am the bread of life. Your fathers ate the manna in the wilderness, and are dead. This is the bread which comes down from heaven, that one may eat of it and not die. I am the living bread which came down from heaven. If anyone eats of this bread, he will live forever; and the bread that I shall give is My flesh, which I shall give for the life of the world."

After the Tabernacle was built, the Israelites had God-given protection. The Israelites were given shade from the sun, the cloud during the day, and warmth, the fire by night. In the New Testament, Jesus said, "I am the good shepherd. The good shepherd gives His life for the sheep." (John 10:11)

- **The Israelites, the church in the wilderness, went from being slaves in Egypt to being God's special people.**

Deuteronomy 32:9–10 For the LORD's portion is His people; Jacob is the place of His inheritance. He found him in a desert land and in the wasteland, a howling wilderness; He encircled him, He instructed him, He kept him as the apple of His eye.

The Church is going from being satan's captives to being members of God's family.

1 Peter 2:9–10 "But you are a chosen generation, a royal priesthood, a holy nation, His own special people, that you may proclaim the praises of Him who called you out of darkness into His marvelous light; who once were not a people but are now the people of God, who had not obtained mercy but now have obtained mercy." We need to embrace that truth and stop thinking of ourselves as sinners saved by grace. Yes we are sinners saved by grace but once we are saved we become God's own special people. The Apostle Paul writes: "What then shall we say to these things? If God is for us, who can be against us? He who did not spare His own Son, but delivered Him up for us all, how shall He not with Him also freely give us all things?" (Romans 8:31–32)

> *The Church is going from being satan's captives to God's family.*

- **The Israelites, the church in the wilderness, were on a special journey.**

The Israelites were on a journey from someplace (Egypt) to someplace (Canaan's Land). They weren't brought out of the bondage of Egypt so they could wander around until they died. Death happened because of their unbelief and rebellion but death was not God's original plan. God had a specific destiny for them - Canaan's Land - and God directed their path. "And the LORD went before them by day in a pillar of cloud to lead the way, and by night in a pillar of fire to give them light, so as to go by day and night." (Exodus 13:21)

The Church is also on a journey from someplace (living in the world of sin) to someplace (that where He is, there we may be also). That journey is expressed in many ways in New Testament Scripture.

In Ephesians 4:11–13 this journey is expressed as a time of training and growth. "And He Himself (Jesus Christ) gave some to be apostles, some prophets, some evangelists, and some pastors and teachers, for the equipping of the saints for the work of ministry, for the edifying of the body of Christ, till we all come to the unity of the faith and of the knowledge of the Son of God, to a perfect man, to the measure of the stature of the fullness of Christ."

In Ephesians 5:26–27 this journey is expressed as sanctification through the work of the Word of God. "...that He might sanctify and cleanse her with the washing of water by the word, that He might present her to Himself a glorious church, not having spot or wrinkle or any such thing, but that she should be holy and without blemish."

In 2 Corinthians 3:18 this journey is expressed as transformation over time. "But we all, with unveiled face, beholding as in a mirror the glory of the Lord, are being transformed into the same image from glory to glory, just as by the Spirit of the Lord."

In Revelation chapters 2 and 3 this journey is described as learning to listen to God and overcoming problems and obstacles in our lives. "He who has an ear, let him hear what the Spirit says to the churches. To him who overcomes I will give to eat from the tree of life, which is in the midst of the Paradise of God." (Revelation 2:7)

In Revelation 19:6–7 this journey is expressed as a bride readying herself for her wedding. "And I heard, as it were, the voice of a great multitude, as the sound of many waters and as the sound of mighty thunderings, saying, 'Alleluia! For the Lord God Omnipotent reigns! Let us be glad and rejoice and give Him glory, for the marriage of the Lamb has come, and His wife has made herself ready.'"

It took Israel 40 years to make the journey. The Christian's journey takes time, too. It is a time for growth. We are going from newborn babies to mature sons and daughters of God. There are important stops along the way and it takes a while; the journey is important but it is not the final goal.

- **God had a plan, a destination, for Israel.**

God had a plan for Israel as they left Egypt for Canaan's Land. God's plan was about much more than the journey. Yes, they learned a lot on the journey but the journey had a destination; a destination predetermined by God before the journey even began.

The Church is on a journey and we have a lot of growing to do on this journey and as with Israel, God's plan for the Church is more than the journey. Salvation is the starting point of this journey but like most journeys, there is a destination. The destination isn't limited to Heaven, or the New Heavens and the New Earth.

This destiny is so grand that it has been described in a multitude of ways. In Romans 8:29 this destiny is described as being conformed to the image of Jesus. "For whom He foreknew, He also predestined to be conformed to the image of His Son, that He might be the firstborn among many brethren." In Ephesians it's described as becoming an instrument of showing forth God's awesome wisdom. "...and to make all see what is the fellowship of the mystery, which from the beginning of the ages has been hidden in God who created all things through Jesus Christ; to the intent that now the manifold wisdom of God might be made known by the church to the principalities and powers in the heavenly places, according to the eternal purpose which He accomplished in Christ Jesus our Lord." (Ephesians 3:9–11) In Colossians it's described as Christ in you the hope of glory. "...the mystery which has been hidden from ages and from generations, but now has been revealed to His saints. To them God willed to make known what are the riches of the glory of this mystery among the Gentiles: which is

Christ in you, the hope of glory." (1:26–27) And in the book of Revelation this destiny is described as sons of God. "And He said to me, 'It is done! I am the Alpha and the Omega, the Beginning and the End. I will give of the fountain of the water of life freely to him who thirsts. He who overcomes shall inherit all things, and I will be his God and he shall be My son.'" (21:6–7)

DISCUSSION QUESTIONS FOR CHAPTER 5

Can you give a brief description of the parallel between the journey of the Israelites from Egypt to Canaan's land and your journey from salvation to heaven?

How can you use Israel's journey to help others understand that our Christian life just begins at salvation and that God has a great purpose for each of His children?

How can you challenge other Christians to continue to grow in their relationship with God?

Questions: What are leaks and garlic, distractions and time-wasters, that should be laid aside in your life so you can run God's race more efficiently?

Discuss Jesus being the bread and water for believers.

How are we more than sinners saved by grace and are now God's own special people?

What impacted you as you read about the journey of Christians from new babes to mature sons and daughters of God?

THE TABERNACLE OF MOSES

Continuing with the theme of "The Church in the Wilderness"; one of the most important events that took place in "The Church in the Wilderness" was the building of what is commonly referred to as the Tabernacle of Moses. As I was thinking about the traits of the Church, as listed in chapter 4, the Tabernacle of Moses came to mind. I began to see connections between those traits and the furniture in the Tabernacle.

Over the past number of years, my wife and I have been blessed to be invited to minister in Singapore and Indonesia numerous times. The first time I was invited I was asked to teach a short seminar on the Tabernacle of Moses. I only had a few hours and since this is such a large topic I asked for some clarification. I was

> *Our journey as Christians starts with Jesus and ends with Jesus.*

told by the brother who invited me that he remembered the teaching from years ago while attending our Church and that he wanted to instill in the young people in his Church that salvation isn't the end of the journey but just the beginning. I trust that you can see that we really are on a journey that takes us from the Gate to the Mercy Seat. Each piece of furniture in the Tabernacle is vitally important but we aren't supposed to stop until we have entered into the very Holy of Holies, into the presence of God Himself. Our journey as Christians starts with Jesus and ends with Jesus. "'I am the Alpha and the Omega, the Beginning and the End,' says the Lord, 'who is and who was and who is to come, the Almighty.'" (Revelation 1:8)

One of the most important lessons that we need to learn from the Tabernacle is that our life in Christ is a journey; it has a beginning, a middle, and an end. In Old Testament times, an Israelite who sinned brought his offering to the Outer Court to be offered to God on the altar to pay for his sin. He recognized his need for forgiveness and came to make the sacrifice. He wore his normal clothing, he had the sun shining on him, he was surrounded by white linen, dirt was under his feet; he had added forgiveness to his normal existence. However, only the priests could enter into the next level. The priests had to be sanctified (which is to be set apart for service to God). They had to put on special garments to function as priests when they went into the Holy Place, the first part of the actual Tabernacle. There they were surrounded by walls made of wood covered with gold. In the Holy Place the curtains and the ceiling were woven with cherubim, the light they had was from the Golden Lampstand and the only connection they had with the world was the dirt they walked on. Then when the High Priest went into the Holy of Holies, the walls covered with gold and the curtain and the ceiling continued to surround him but now the only light he had to see by was the actual Glory of God that filled the room. These priests were clothed with Holy garments and surrounded with the Glory of God. They had stopped drawing their identity from the world around them and had begun to identify with the Glory of God.

Can you see the progression? An individual goes from a sinner bringing a sacrifice to pay for his sin, to a priest set apart to God clothed in Holy garments surrounded by the Glory of God, to the High Priest who enters into the very presence of God Himself.

> ***Stop identifying with the world and begin to identify with the Glory of God!***

The Tabernacle of Moses helps us see that as Christians, we start off with salvation but we are not supposed to stop there. We are to be sanctified as priests. (1 Corinthians 6:11 and Revelation 1:6) We are to put Jesus on as a Holy garment. (Romans 13:14, Galatians 3:27, and Colossians 3:10-14) We are to live in the presence and Glory of God. (Ephesians 1:3, 2:6) We are not to be earthly minded but to be mindful of heavenly things. (Colossians 3:1-2) We are to focus on the Kingdom of God (Mathew 6:33) so that we can fulfill all of the purposes of God here in this world as we press toward God's eternal kingdom.

THE TABERNACLE OF MOSES

Here we have a diagram of the Tabernacle of Moses. It gives us a quick overview of the structure. The Israelite brought his offering through the Gate on the east end of the courtyard. He took the sacrifice to the priest at the Brazen Altar and the priest offered the sacrifice there. Only priests would go beyond the Brazen Altar and only the High Priest could go into the Holy of Holies.

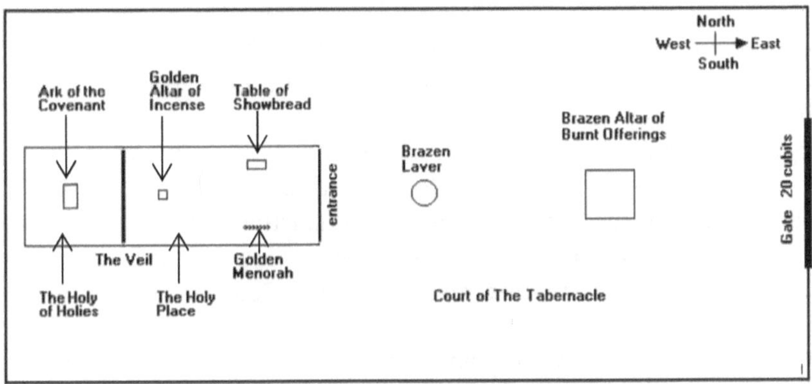

In the Court of the Tabernacle (also called the Outer Court) there were:
> The Brazen (Brass) Altar of Sacrifice
> The Brazen (Brass) Laver

In the first room of the Tabernacle (also called The Holy Place) there were:
> The Golden Lampstand
> The Table of Showbread
> The Altar of Incense

In the second room of the Tabernacle (also called The Holy of Holies or the Most Holy Place) there were:
> The Ark of the Covenant
> The Mercy Seat

The Tabernacle of Moses depicts people in different roles (i.e. Israelites, priests and the high priest) and The Law tells us how they relate to the different pieces of furniture and places in the Tabernacle. This Tabernacle was where God said He would dwell. (Exodus 25:8; 29:46-47) Today the Church (not the place but the people) is the dwelling place of God (1 Cor. 3:16, 2 Cor. 6:16, Eph. 2:20-22) and we will examine the relationship between the different pieces of furniture in Moses' Tabernacle and our growth from brand new babies in Christ into mature sons and daughters of God in the following pages.

AN OVERVIEW OF THE FURNITURE IN THE TABERNACLE OF MOSES

There are many wonderful books dealing with the types and shadows (insights into New Testament Spiritual meanings of things) found in the Tabernacle of Moses. Details of this Tabernacle are found in Exodus chapters 25 through 30. We will not attempt a deep study here, but one thing that needs to be pointed out from the Tabernacle of Moses, starting at the gate and ending at the Mercy Seat, is that the Tabernacle is a picture of our journey from sinner to mature son/daughter of God.

The Tabernacle as a whole represents Jesus and each piece of furniture represents different aspects of Jesus' ministry to the Church. This furniture also represents changes in our lives as we grow as Christians.

Before we enter the Tabernacle, we need to look at the symbolic meaning of three of the main materials used in its construction.

BRASS – Brazen Altar and Brazen Laver

Brass symbolizes judgment against sin. (Deuteronomy 28:13-23 KJV)

WOOD – Posts to hold up the outer curtain, to make the frame of the Brazen Altar, and to make the walls and some furniture in the Holy Place and Most Holy Place

Wood in the Old Testament is often a symbol for humanity. (Psalms 1:3; Psalms 52:8) Acacia wood (the wood used in the Tabernacle) grows in the desert and *"is resistant to decay because the tree deposits in the heartwood many ... substances which are preservatives and render the wood unpalatable to insects making the wood dense and difficult to be penetrated by water and other decay agents."*[1] The Septuagint version of the Old Testament actually translates the word as "incorruptible" or "non-decaying" wood. The Apostle Paul says this about the flesh of Jesus. "For what the law could not do in that it was weak through the flesh, God did by sending His own Son in the likeness of sinful flesh, on account of sin: He condemned sin in the flesh." (Romans 8:3) We know that Jesus was in the flesh but did not sin. (Hebrews 4:15) Isaiah describes Jesus as, "a root out of dry ground." (Isaiah 53:2) So, considering all the above, acacia wood is a fitting symbol for the sinless, incorruptible humanity of Jesus.

GOLD – To make some of the furniture, to cover the wood furniture, and to line the boards used to make the walls in the Tabernacle proper

Because of gold's value and its incorruptibility, gold is often seen as symbolic of God and the nature of God.

> *The Tabernacle is a picture of our journey from sinner to mature son/daughter of God.*

1.   *http://ww2.odu.edu/~lmusselm/plant/bible/acacia.php/* © *2006 Old Dominion University, Norfolk, VA 23529*

THE GATE
Jesus the door

*"Then Jesus said to them again, 'Most assuredly,
I say to you, I am the door of the sheep.'"*
John 10:7

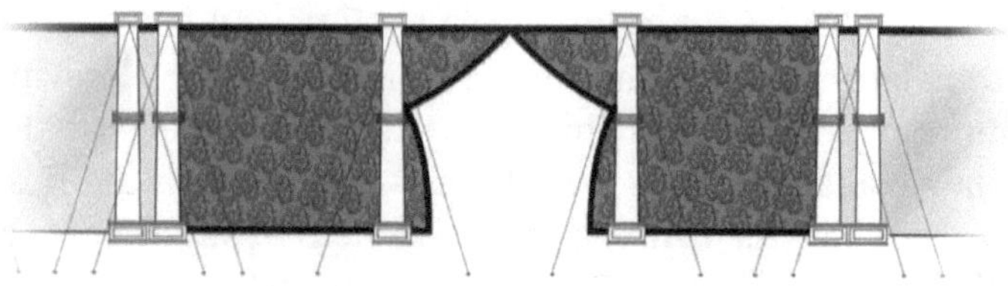

Since Jesus is the gate to the sheepfold, there is only one way to God and that is through Jesus Christ. Everyone begins outside the gate. Romans 3:23 (KJV) explains it this way. "For all have sinned, and come short of the glory of God...." What is this glory of God that we have all come short of?

The word glory, as applied to God, has many meanings; but the primary meaning I want to look at here is found in Exodus 33:18-34:7. Moses asks God to let him see God's glory. God responded in a rather unusual way. He said: "I will make all My goodness pass before you, and I will proclaim the name of the LORD before you. I will be gracious to whom I will be gracious, and I will have compassion on whom I will have compassion." God equated His glory with His goodness and His name. In the Old Testament a person's name spoke of his nature and character. (Consider Abram's and Jacob's name changes.) God is telling us here that His glory is not just a brilliance or a great cloud but is tied to His nature and character. We also see God's glory is tied to His presence when God's glory was to pass by "the LORD descended in the cloud and stood with him there...." (Exodus 34:5)

> *God equated His glory with His goodness and His name. In the Old Testament a person's name spoke of his nature and character.*

Why is this important here? Because sin is connected with coming short of the glory of God. We don't have to wait until we are born again to see God's glory. God's glory is revealed in His creation, "The heavens declare the glory of God; And the firmament shows His handiwork," (Psalm 19:1) and "The whole earth is full of His glory!" (Isaiah 6:3b) But to partake of His glory requires new birth. At salvation we begin to see His glory, but the fullness of His glory (think: nature, character, presence) is not revealed until we reach the Holiest of Holies where God said He would meet with His people above the Mercy Seat. Until we enter that realm we are not necessarily sinning but we are still coming short of the glory of God that we have been designed to partake of. We have only just begun our journey when we approach the Gate.

Passing through the Gate, the first thing we see is the Brazen Altar of Sacrifice.

BRAZEN ALTAR OF SACRIFICE
Jesus our Savior

"Behold, the lamb of God who takes away the sins of the world."
John 1:29 (KJV)

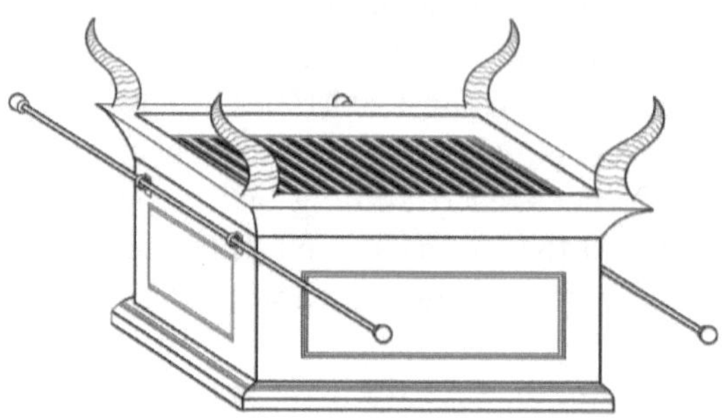

The Brazen Altar of Sacrifice was made of wood covered with brass. It was used for the offering of sacrifices for the sins of the people. The altar had four brass horns, one on each corner. The Altar speaks of judgment for and the forgiveness of sin through the shedding of blood. Jesus is described as our "horn of salvation." (Luke 1:68-69) The Brazen Altar reveals the dedication and suffering of Jesus to bring atonement for us. Jesus was the complete burnt offering offered "once for all." (Hebrews 10:10; 1 Corinthians 15:3)

Because of what Jesus did on the cross, the veil between the Holy Place and the Holy of Holies has been ripped from the top to the bottom. Access has been opened into the very presence of God.

Under the Old Covenant only the priests were able to go past this altar. However, in the New Covenant we have been made priests unto God by the blood of Jesus. (1 Peter 2:5 & 9; Revelation 1:5-6)

Our journey as Christians has begun; we have been bought with the blood of Jesus, have been born again, and have become a part of the family of God. (Ephesians 2:19 NLT) What a power-filled beginning! But, just like being born into the human family, we don't begin as adults, we begin as babies. (1 Peter 2:2)

In the natural, we don't want our children to stop growing before they become adults, so likewise in the Spirit, God wants us to grow. (1 Peter 2:2; Philippians 1:6) Our journey is not the main point; this journey has a destination prepared for us by God Himself. Romans 8:29 talks about that destination: "For whom He foreknew, He also predestined to be conformed to the image of His Son, that He might be the

> *Under the Old Covenant, there was an unwritten "Keep out!" sign over the curtain leading to the Holy of Holies. Under the New Covenant, there is an unwritten "Please Come In; I have been waiting for you!" sign on the now torn curtain.*

firstborn among many brethren." We have to start at the Brazen Altar where Jesus is the sacrifice for our sins, otherwise Jesus calls us "thieves and robbers." (John 10:1) But our journey is not supposed to stop there.

Because of what Jesus did on the cross, the veil between the Holy Place and the Holy of Holies has been ripped from the top to the bottom. (Mark 15:38) Access has been opened into the very presence of God (Holy of Holies). Oh, the wonders of the New and Better Covenant! Under the Old Covenant, there was an invisible sign over the veil into the Holy of Holies that read "Keep out on penalty of Death." Only the high priest was able to go in and he could only enter in on one day a year and only after making sacrifices for his own sins. Any other entry resulted in the death of the one who entered. After Jesus' sacrifice, there is a new invisible sign that says: "Welcome, please come in!" (Hebrews 4:16) Remember, the veil was torn from top to bottom (Matthew 27:51) showing that it was God, Himself, through the sacrifice of His Son that opened the way for us to freely enter into His Presence. However, we cannot go from the Brazen Altar (salvation) into the Holy of Holies (the fullness of God) without passing by and participating in the other pieces of furniture along the way.

So, let us continue this journey. After the Brazen Altar we come to the Brazen Laver. The Brazen Laver is a very interesting piece of furniture.

The Brazen Laver was a large uncovered container of water and it speaks first of water baptism.

You might not know that, if you are a Hindu, no one cares if you add the worship of Jesus to your millions of other gods but when you are baptized, you proclaim that Jesus is the only way and you can be cut off from your Hindu family. Likewise, our lives as Christians is not just adding Jesus to our daily routine but our lives are to be sanctified, set apart as we immerse ourselves in the very presence and Glory of God.

The primary purpose of the Laver was for the priests to wash away the dirt and grime that soiled them daily because of the sacrifices and the dirt they walked on. So, along with water baptism, this Laver also represents the washing of water of the Word (Eph.5:26-27), an outer cleansing of the contamination that comes from contact with the world. This is not dealing with the sins of our past; they are forgiven by God and blotted out by God at salvation. This cleansing deals with the reality that we live in a fallen world where we can be influenced by the evil of this world and need to daily cleanse ourselves with the washing of the water of the Word. We are new creations in Christ Jesus; we are not supposed to conform again to this world. (Romans 12:2) We look into the water of the Word and see the contamination, and we wash with the water of the Word for cleansing. Let me give an example of this concept. In the current political climate, there is a lot of hatred toward those who disagree with one's particular point of view. When we are exposed to that over and over again in the news and in conversations around us, we can begin to react to people disagreeing with us with the same kind of anger and hatred. If we stay in the Word on a daily basis, the Spirit of God that flows in and through His Word washes that animosity out of our hearts and we act out of love to our fellow man rather than reacting to their anger, hatred, etc.

The brass for this Laver came from the mirrors of the Israeli women. (Exodus 38:8) It is by looking into the Laver that we learn what the new creation is like. When we look into the Bible, we "Behold as in a mirror, the glory of the Lord...." (2 Corinthians 3:18) When we read God's Word and as we are taught by the ministry, we learn what it means to be a child of God. Remember, when we are born again, we are a new creation but because we are still learning and growing, we need to be taught what it means to live as a child of God. Here at the Laver we also learn the importance of being "doers of the Word, and not hearers only." (James 1:22-25)

Continuing our journey, we have to go through the entrance into the Tabernacle proper. The first room we enter is called the Holy Place. When we go through the curtain of the entrance, the first thing that draws our attention is the bright light of the Lampstand reflecting off the gold that covered everything made of wood in the Holy Place.

THE LAMPSTAND
Jesus our Light

*"I am the light of the world. He who follows Me
shall not walk in darkness, but have the light of life."*
John 8:12b

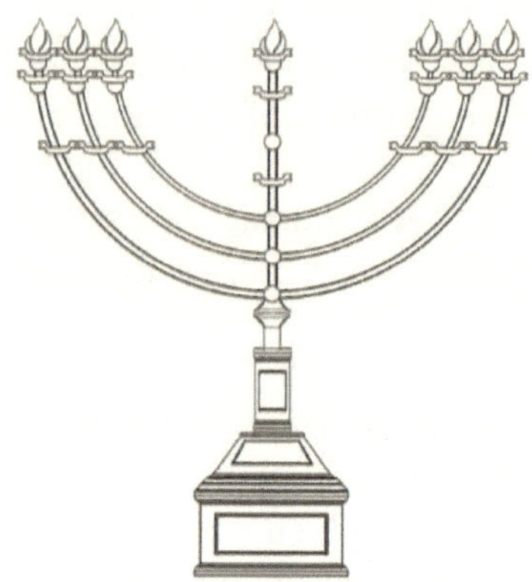

The Lampstand was thought to look similar to a very large traditional Menorah candlestick. It was not a candlestick but a lampstand. It didn't hold candles; it held oil and the seven lamps had wicks.

The Lampstand was one of only two pieces of furniture in the Tabernacle that was pure gold. The other piece of furniture made of pure gold was the Mercy Seat. The Lampstand was made from one piece of gold and beaten into the final shape. This Lampstand was covered with beautiful, intricate designs. The Lampstand was considered to be the most beautiful and ornamental of all of the pieces of the furniture in the Tabernacle. Because of the heavy covering over the Tabernacle proper, it was the only light in the Holy Place.

> *The Lampstand was considered
> to be the most beautiful and
> ornamental of all of the pieces of
> the furniture in the Tabernacle.*

The light of the Lampstand is a direct picture of the Holy Spirit. (Acts 2:1-4) The J. B. Phillips translation of the New Testament reads this way: "He will baptize you with the fire of the Holy Spirit." (Matthew 3:11) So, as we press on in our journey in God, we come face to face with the Holy Spirit. We cannot overstate the value of the Holy Spirit in our lives as we grow in God. Jesus called Him the Comforter, the Teacher, the Spirit of Truth. (John 14:26; John 16:13) The Holy Spirit is instrumental in guiding our lives as we continue this journey. (Acts 10:19-20; Acts 16:6; Romans 8:4)

If we desire to explore the depths of the Word of God, we desperately need the light of the Holy Spirit as we read God's Word because Jesus said that it's the Holy Spirit that will guide us into all truth. (John 16:13; 1 Corinthians 2:13; 1 John 2:27)

The Lampstand had a central shaft called "His branch." (Exodus 37:17) This shaft speaks to us of

> *We cannot overstate the value of the Holy Spirit in our lives as we grow in God.*

Christ. He is the center of all things to the Church. Everything originates from Christ. Jesus is the head of all things to the Church. (Ephesians 1:22) The Lampstand had six branches (the number of man) with three branches on either side. The Lampstand was formed from one piece of gold. This brings us to the understanding that not only is Jesus the source of everything to the Church but that we are one with Him, flesh of His flesh, and bone of His bone. (Ephesians 5:30)

The Lampstand was of beaten gold, shaped by hammer blows (beaten - Exodus 37:36; Numbers 8:4) which speaks of the suffering of Christ. (Hebrews 2:10b; Isaiah 53:4-5) The branches were shaped by the same process. (Matthew 5:10 & 11; Colossians 1:24; Philippians 1:29) Thus, the Lampstand as a whole speaks of Christ and His Church. (Revelation 2 & 3)

As we look at the other side of the Holy Place, we see the light of the Holy Spirit shining brightly on the Table of Showbread.

TABLE OF SHOWBREAD
Jesus our Sustenance

"And Jesus said to them, 'I am the bread of life.
He who comes to Me shall never hunger, and he who
believes in Me shall never thirst.'"
John 6:35

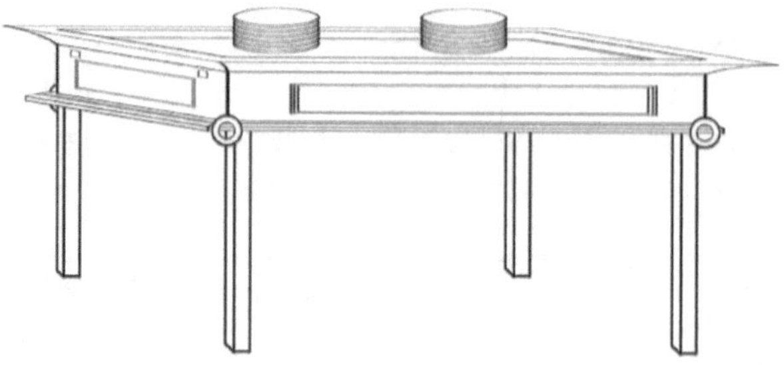

The Table of Showbread was a wooden table overlaid with gold that had 12 loaves of bread, in two stacks of six loaves, placed on it. Jesus is the "Bread of Life." (John 6:35 & 48) Jesus is the "Word made flesh", as we partake of Him, He becomes a part of who we are. (John 1:14 & 6:51)

When we are "washed with the water of the Word" at the Laver, we are cleansed from the daily contamination that we pick up by just living in a fallen world. I mentioned this before but there is an important distinction between the washing of the Word that takes place at the Laver and the eating of the Word that takes place at the Table of Showbread. To help describe this difference let's consider the time Jesus was washing His disciples' feet. When Jesus came to Peter, Peter said to Him, "'You shall never wash my feet!' Jesus answered him, 'If I do not wash you, you have no part with Me.' Simon Peter said to Him, 'Lord, not my feet only, but also my hands and my head!' Jesus said to him, 'He who is bathed needs only to wash his feet, but is completely clean; and you are clean....'" (John 13:8–10a) During the time of Jesus' sojourn on the earth people wore sandals and walked on dirt roads. Even someone newly bathed who had to walk to a friend's house would get his feet dirty. That is why the custom was to wash a guest's feet, especially when he came to dine. Jesus was saying (my paraphrase): "Peter, you are clean because of your faith in me, but because of your close

84

contact with the world (dirt) I need to wash your feet (that which touches the dirt)." Daily contact with the world is washed away by daily reading the Word of God.

The washing of the water of the Word as relating to the Laver speaks of cleansing the outer man. Eating the Bread of Life also speaks of the Word but as it relates to the Table of Showbread. It is the Word of God working in the inner man, the law of God being written on the tablets of our hearts. (Jeremiah 31:33 & Hebrews 8:10) An interesting example of this took place early in my ministry. A young man in our Church went on a juice diet. He happened to pick carrot juice and after a week or so his skin actually began to turn orange. The old saying, "You are what you eat" also applies in the Spirit world.

When we eat of the Bread of Life that is on the Table of Showbread, God's Word gets into our heart. Then His Word becomes part of our nature and changes us from the inside out. The more of God's Word that gets into our heart, the better we understand His Word and that results in us bearing Spiritual fruit. (Matthew 13:18-23; James 1:21; Galatians 5:22)

In Exodus 25:30 (ESV, TBN, NLT), this bread is called the "Presence Bread." Again, this is a picture of our relationship with Jesus. "For He Himself has said, 'I will never leave you nor forsake you.'" (Hebrews 13:5b)

As we continue on past the Table of Showbread, heading toward the entrance to the Holiest of Holies, we come to the Altar of Incense.

ALTAR OF INCENSE
Jesus our Intercessor

*"Therefore He is also able to save to the uttermost
those who come to God through Him, since He always
lives to make intercession for them."*
Hebrews 7:25

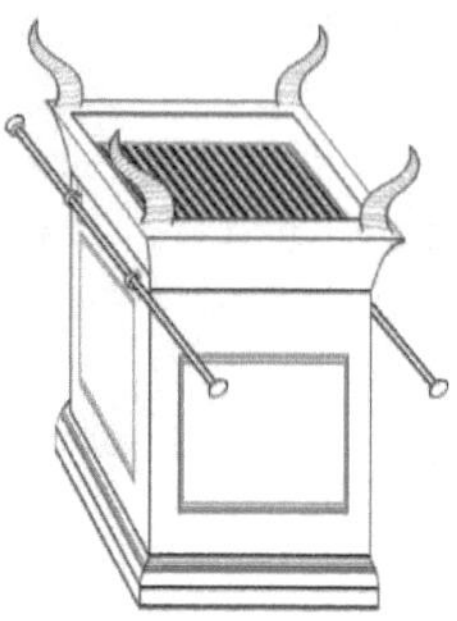

The Altar of Incense was made of wood covered with gold. On this Altar a special incense was burned in worship to God. (2 Chronicles 32:12) From Psalms 141:1 & 2 and Revelation 8:3-4 we learn that the burning of incense not only represents worship but it also represents prayer. So, this piece of furniture speaks to us of prayer and praise and worship.

It is interesting that the Altar of Incense was located right in front of the entrance to the Holy of Holies. The position of this Altar reveals to us that, if we want to press into the very presence of God, we must devote ourselves to prayer and praise and worship. Psalms 100:4 tells us that we enter His gates with thanksgiving and His courts with praise. There, in His presence, we can boldly bring our petitions to Him.

Finally, our journey has led us to the entrance into the very Holy of Holies. We don't have to stop here in front of the final curtain and wait for that special day that only came around once each year; that day when the High Priest went to minister behind the veil. We are able to walk right on through the veil because it was ripped from top to bottom when Jesus died on the cross. (Matthew 27:50-51) We can freely move from the Holy Place into the Holy of Holies.

I mentioned that under the Old Covenant only the high priest was able to go into the Holy of Holies and He could only go in on one day a year and only after making sacrifices for his own sins. But, in the New Covenant, after Jesus died for our sins, the veil was torn from the top to the bottom and there is no separation between the Holy Place and the Holy of Holies. (Matthew 27:51) Now, we can boldly come into the presence of the Creator of the universe, the throne room of God Himself. (Hebrews 4:16 and 10:19)

When we enter the throne room of God, we come face to face with the glory of God as revealed in the final two pieces of furniture; the Ark of the Covenant and the Mercy Seat. These fit together to look like one piece of furniture but God talks about them as being a box, the Ark of the Covenant, and the lid of that box, the Mercy Seat.

An interesting side note: the Outer Court had the light of the sun, the Holy Place had the light of the Lampstand but there was no source of light in the Holy of Holies except the Glory of God. (See the outline of the Tabernacle at the beginning of this section.)

ARK OF THE COVENANT
Jesus fully God and fully man
*"In the beginning was the Word, and the Word was
with God, and the Word was God."*
"And the Word became flesh and dwelt among us...."
John 1:1 & John 1:14a

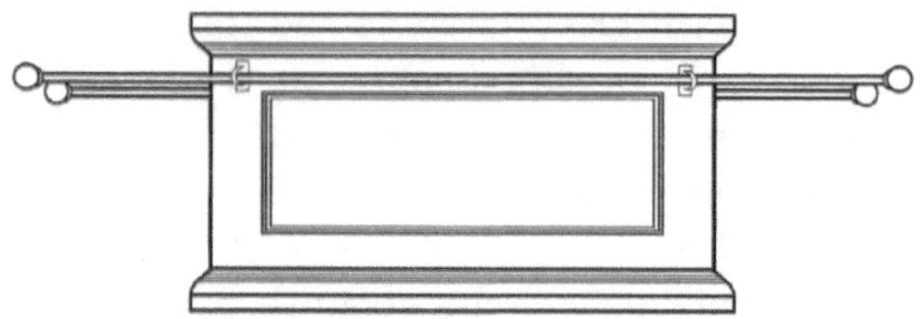

The Ark of the Covenant was a box made of acacia wood. The
Mercy Seat was solid gold and sat on top of the Ark of the
Covenant. These looked like one piece of furniture but were in fact
two distinct pieces of furniture.

A very interesting thing about acacia wood was that it had lots of
long sharp thorns on it. The only time Jesus was crowned in His
earthly life was with a crown of thorns.

As the Israelites continued to craft the Ark, the acacia wood was
covered inside and outside with gold. Gold and wood don't mix so
we see the Ark of the Covenant symbolizes Jesus, fully God and
fully man.

Since the Ark was covered within and without with gold, no matter
how you looked at the box all you could see was gold. No matter
how you look at Jesus, His outward actions or inward motives, you
see God! In the book of John, Jesus says, "... He who has seen Me
has seen the Father...." (John 14:9)

> **In the presence of
> God, we are changed
> into the image of His
> Son.**

A crown of gold was shaped around
the upper edge to complete the Ark.
(Exodus 25:11) The word translated
here for crown is only used ten times,
and it was used when describing the
molding of pure gold that went around the upper edge of the Table

of Showbread, the Altar of Incense, and the Ark of the Covenant. Modern Bible translations use the word molding or ring instead of crown. Since this is the only place this Hebrew word is used in the Bible, there is no way to compare usage in a different context. So, I went to "THE HOLY SCRIPTURES" copyright 1917 by The Jewish Publication Society of America. They translate this word as crown the ten times it shows up in Exodus. I like the word crown because this molding or ring of gold was only placed on those pieces of furniture that were made of wood covered with gold. The Word was made flesh and He dwelt among us. (John 1:1 & 14) And however Jesus expressed Himself to us in this world He was always King of kings, crowned with glory and honor. (Hebrews 2:9; Revelation 19:16)

In the Ark were the Tablets of the Law that God gave Moses, a golden bowl of manna, and Aaron's rod that budded. The Ark represents Jesus Christ in His life on this earth. Jesus fulfilled the Law, He was the Bread of Life, and He had authority given Him by God. Jesus was both God (gold) and man (wood). The Ark also carried the presence of God, and Jesus was God in the flesh. (1 Samuel 4:4; John 1:1)

Entering into the Holy of Holies and facing this Ark, we begin to realize we carry the presence of the Lord everywhere we go. Here, in the presence of God Himself, we are changed into the image of His Son. Here the New Covenant is fully realized as the law of God is written on our hearts (not stone tablets); as we live on the "hidden manna", and as we walk in our authority in Jesus Christ.

And right there, sitting on top of the Ark of the Covenant is the crowning glory of the Tabernacle, the Mercy Seat.

MERCY SEAT
Jesus the Presence of God
Jesus the Glory of God

"(Jesus) who being the brightness of His glory
and the express image of His person."
Hebrews 1:3a

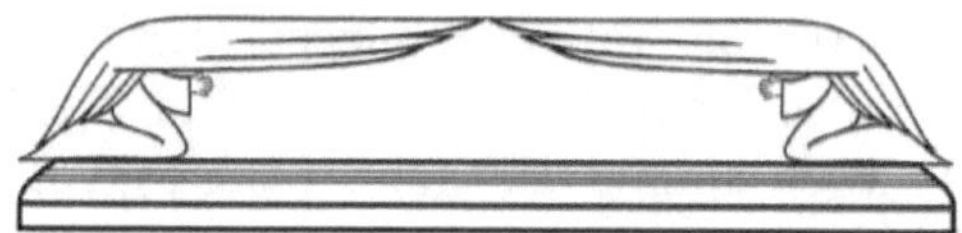

The Mercy Seat was a lid for the Ark of the Covenant and it is made of pure gold; gold that was beaten into the proper shape. The Mercy Seat was not simply a lid or top but it was the most important piece of furniture in the whole Tabernacle. The Holy of Holies is actually described as "the place of the Mercy Seat" in 1 Chronicles 28:11 (KJV).

On the top of the Mercy Seat were two Cherubim of gold, one at each end. These Cherubim faced each other, and their wings stretched to cover the Mercy Seat. (Exodus 25:20; Hebrews 9:5)

"And there I will meet with you, and I will speak with you from above the mercy seat, from between the two cherubim which are on the ark of the Testimony, about everything which I will give you in commandment to the children of Israel." (Exodus 25:22; Numbers 7:89) Isn't it wonderful that God said that He would meet with us above the Mercy Seat! God didn't say He would meet us at the judgment seat. There is a judgment seat, but God meets with His children at the Mercy Seat. When we were sinners our sins demanded judgment but to get to the Mercy Seat we had to start at the Brazen Altar where our sins were washed away by the Blood of Jesus! Judgment is past, all our sins have been cast into the sea (Micah 7:18-19), and we meet with God at His Mercy Seat. No wonder, as participants in the New Covenant, we can come boldly before the throne of grace. (Hebrews 4:16)

The Mercy Seat represents God's manifest presence. (Leviticus 16:2) Both Psalms 80:1 and Psalms 99:1 speak of the Mercy Seat as

God's throne, and a king rules from his throne. The Messiah was to be called Immanuel, God with us. (Isaiah 7:14) Who is that? Jesus! This is pointed out when the writer of Hebrews used the Greek word HIASTERION Strong's: 2435; [hilasterion]. This word is translated Mercy Seat in Hebrews 9:5. There are only two occurrences in the New Testament. KJV translates it as propitiation once, and mercy seat once.

In the other occurrence of that word in the New Testament, the Apostle Paul was referring to none other than Jesus Christ Himself in Romans 3:24–25, "... Christ Jesus, whom God set forth as a propitiation by His blood...." We could just as correctly translate this as, "Christ Jesus, whom God set forth as the Mercy Seat...."

Additionally, in 1 Samuel 4:21-22 the Ark of the Covenant and the Mercy Seat together are referred to as being the carrier of God's Glory.

This picture of the Glory of God is definitely pointing to Jesus. John declares that Jesus was the Word made flesh, and that they beheld His Glory. (John 1:14) The writer of Hebrews says that Jesus was the glory of God, and the express image of God's person. (Hebrews 1:3) Paul, in 1 Corinthians 2:8, calls Jesus "the Lord of Glory", and then again, in 2 Corinthians 4:6, Paul says that we see "the light of the knowledge of the glory of God in the face of Jesus Christ."

In the Holy of Holies we see a fulfillment of the Scripture that declares: "All of us! Nothing between us and God, our faces

> *It is God's intent that even though we start out this journey as babies in Christ we do not stay there. He has an "end" in store for us.*

shining with the brightness of his face. And so we are transfigured much like the Messiah, our lives gradually becoming brighter and more beautiful as God enters our lives and we become like Him." (2 Corinthians 3:18 TMB)

Here in the Holy of Holies we have reached the place that this earthly journey comes to its end. I love the Greek word used in 1 Peter 1:9: "Receiving the <u>end</u> of your faith, even the salvation of your souls." This word end in the King James Bible is the Greek word, [telos], Strong's: 5056. It means the expected culmination of a thing's beginning. For example, the telos of an acorn is a full-grown oak tree bearing acorns. It is God's intent that even though we start out this journey as babies in Christ we do not stay there. He has an end in store for us. Jeremiah 29:11 (KJV) states: "For I know the thoughts that I think toward you, saith the LORD, thoughts of peace, and not of evil, to give you an expected end."

By the grace of God and the power of His Holy Spirit, that end is to become just like Jesus. (Romans 8:29; Ephesians 4:13; Colossians 3:10; Philippians 3:21) Selah!

The symbolism in the Tabernacle is marvelous. The Outer Court was the place of forgiveness of sins (salvation). The Holy Place was the place of service to God (Christian growth). The Holy of Holies was the place of meeting with God face to face (fellowship and relationship).

What Jesus does for the sinner is wonderful, and the steps to full Salvation are clearly symbolized in the Tabernacle furniture! A sinner makes a decision to take a sacrifice through the <u>Gate,</u> recognizing that they have sinned and fallen short of the glory of God. This sinner receives forgiveness at the <u>Brazen Altar</u> through the substitutionary sacrifice of Jesus Christ. Then, at the <u>Brazen Laver,</u> he finds cleansing and change. Through the curtain he gets a glimpse of the light from the <u>Lampstand,</u> and he is drawn into the Holy Place where opening before him is a whole new level of relationship to God. In the Holy Place he begins to grow in the knowledge and power of the Holy Spirit, and begins to become more like Jesus at the <u>Table of Showbread</u>. At the <u>Altar of Incense,</u>

this maturing Christian begins to find delight in prayer and worship as he changes from being self-centered to being Christ-centered. Then, as he moves on into the Holy of Holies, he delights in the presence of God, and here, at the <u>Ark of the Covenant</u>, he truly begins to bear the image of Jesus. Then as this former sinner lifts his eyes to the <u>Mercy Seat</u> he finds unconditional acceptance in Christ Jesus and realizes he is no longer just a sinner saved by grace (Ephesians 2:4 & 5), but he is a saint of the Lord Most High. (Romans 1:7, 1 Corinthians 1:2)

DISCUSSION QUESTIONS FOR CHAPTER 6

Do you see your Christian life more as adding Jesus to your existing lifestyle or more as a changing of your life to follow Jesus?

How has God opened your eyes to see how the Tabernacle is a reflection of the church?

Consider the elements in the Tabernacle. In your own words, express what each piece speaks to you.
Gate –

Brazen Altar –

Brazen Laver –

Lampstand –

Table of Showbread –

Altar of Incense –

Ark of the Covenant –

Mercy Seat –

TRAITS OF THE CHURCH ASSOCIATED WITH THE FURNITURE OF THE TABERNACLE

I have grouped the traits of the Church under the names of the furniture from the Tabernacle of Moses for two reasons: First, I realized the complete list of the traits of the Church was long, cumbersome and repeated some of the traits a number of times. So I looked for a way to arrange the traits into groups of a more manageable size. Second, I see the journey for every believer in the Tabernacle of Moses. As I considered this, I saw how the traits that God desires to be in the New Testament Church correlated with the different pieces of furniture. A few traits appear in more than one place.

BRAZEN ALTAR
Jesus our Savior

The following traits are grouped here because the Brazen Altar represents the awesome love of God and His provision to pay for our salvation through the blood of Jesus.

Traits of the Church	Explanation of the Traits' Fit with Furniture Piece
The Church has purpose.	One aspect of the purpose of the Church is to declare the love of God shown by Jesus dying for our sins.

The message of the Church is Jesus Christ crucified, raised from the dead and living in His Church.	This message begins at the Brazen Altar and concludes at the Mercy Seat.
The Church loves God.	The Brazen Altar shows God's great love and "We love Him because He first loved us." 1 John 4:19
The Church has a firm foundation.	God's great love. "For God so loved the world that He gave His only begotten Son, that whoever believes in Him should not perish but have everlasting life." John 3:16 KJV
The Church is not the building but the people.	Jesus died for humanity, not for a building.
The Church lives in the love of God.	Jesus died because of God's great love for us. John 3:16
The Church belongs to Jesus.	We are bought by the Blood of Jesus. 1 Corinthians 6:20
Individual members of the Church will deny themselves for Christ's sake.	We lay our own lives on the Altar that we might gain His life.
The Church boldly proclaims the need for, and the way of, salvation.	Salvation is by the shed Blood of Jesus.
People don't join the Church, God adds them through new birth.	We are born again when we come to Jesus as our Savior.
The Church loves one another.	We become a part of God's family at salvation and families love each other.
All are welcome to gather together with the Church, but only the saved are added to the Church.	Individuals are added to the Church when they are born again.
Jesus Christ commissioned the Church.	We become part of the Church at the Altar and Jesus said: "... As the Father has sent Me, I also send you." John 20:21

Satan is the enemy of the Church.	The reason we need salvation is because of sin which began with satan's temptation of Adam and Eve.
The Church puts God first.	The first thing you see when you enter the gate is the Brazen Altar.
The Church is victorious.	We have victory over the enemy by the Blood of Jesus.
The Church fears God, not satan.	Because of Jesus' sacrifice on the cross, we have the victory over satan.
The local Church is active.	There is a lot of activity around the Brazen Altar.
The Church is bold to preach and quick to forgive.	The Brazen Altar declared God's forgiveness.
The Church believes in second chances.	Sacrifices were made daily for the sins of the people.
The Church is made up of ordinary people not super-saints.	All of Israel could bring their sacrifices.
The Church refrains from sexual sins.	There is power in the Blood of Jesus to overcome all sin.
God will live in the hearts of individuals in His Church.	God comes into our lives at salvation.
The Church honors those who nurture it both in the natural and Spirit.	In the preaching of the cross, we are continually honoring Jesus for the shedding of His blood.
The Church refrains from contact with idols.	There is only one sacrifice for sin, Jesus.

BRAZEN LAVER
Jesus our Sanctifier

The following traits are grouped here because the Brazen Laver represents the importance of water baptism and our daily cleansing by the washing of the water of the Word.

The Church has purpose.	One aspect of the purpose of the Church is to become spotless by the washing of the water of the Word.

The Church baptizes believers.	The Brazen Laver was filled with water for washing.
The Church teaches the Word of God.	"...that He might sanctify and cleanse her [the Church] with the washing of water by the word." Ephesians 5:26
The local church is active.	The priests were always busy washing.
Church members are honest and people of integrity.	Daily washing with the Word removes the contamination of the world.
The Church is not yet perfect.	Therefore there is a need for continual washing at the Laver.
Until the Church is completed, there will be a great need for love, patience and a lot of forgiveness.	Water from the Brazen Laver was used to wash away every-day filth.
All are welcome to gather together with the Church but only those born again are added to the Church.	Jesus answered, "Most assuredly, I say to you, unless one is born of water and the Spirit, he cannot enter the kingdom of God." John 3:5

LAMPSTAND
Jesus our Light

The following traits are grouped here because the Lampstand represents the power, presence, and teaching ministry of the Holy Spirit.

The Church has purpose.	One aspect of the purpose of the Church is to reveal the light of Jesus to the whole world.
The Church is built on revelation from God.	Revelation comes by the Holy Spirit.
The Church is a Spiritual entity.	The Lampstand represents the Holy Spirit.
The Local Church is a defined body of believers.	The Lampstand had a definite shape with each branch unique.

One person cannot make up a Local Church.	The Lampstand had six branches and one central shaft.
The Church is united.	The Lampstand was formed from one lump of gold.
The Lord dwells in the midst of the Local Church.	Christ was in the midst of the Lampstands in Revelation 2 & 3.
Jesus gives the Church what it needs.	The gifts operate by the Holy Spirit.
Believers are baptized with the Holy Spirit.	The light of the Lampstand represents the Holy Spirit.
Members of the Church speak in new tongues.	Tongues is a gift of the Holy Spirit.
The Church is living, not stagnant.	Fresh oil is put into the Lampstand daily.
The Holy Spirit has preeminence in the Church.	The Lampstand was the only light in the Holy Place.
The Church is endued with supernatural power from God.	Jesus said the Church would be endowed with power when they received the Holy Spirit. Luke 24:49
God's Church has such an abundance of His presence that it will flow out like a river.	Jesus said that out of our bellies would flow rivers of living water, and He was speaking of the Holy Spirit. John 7:38 & 39a
The Church is made up of doers not just hearers.	The oil did not just set in the Lampstand. It was renewed daily as it was burned for light.
The Church has various kinds of ministry.	Seven separate flames were burning on the Lampstand.
The Church does the works that Jesus did and even greater works.	Miracles are only possible with the help of the Holy Spirit.
The Church takes miracles, signs, and wonders into their city.	Light is not to be kept under a basket but to shine for all to see.
The Church is prophetic.	Prophecy is a gift of the Holy Spirit.
The Church is one with God and one with one another.	The central shaft and the branches were all formed out of one piece of gold.

Believers take care of each other.	Each branch of the Lampstand shared the same oil.
The Local Church learns from other Local Churches	The light from each branch was seen by all the other branches.
The Church ministry prays and preaches the Word to the whole world.	Jesus is the Light of the world and that light is to shine to the whole world.
The Church works in Team ministry.	Many lamps were working together to light the Holy Place.
The Church follows Jesus.	"Your word is a lamp to my feet and a light to my path." Psalm 119:105.
The Church practices the Laying on of Hands.	The priests had to work daily with the oil and the wicks to keep them burning correctly.

TABLE OF SHOWBREAD
Jesus our Sustenance

The following traits are grouped here because the Table of Showbread represents the Word of God that we hide in our hearts and the uniqueness as well as the unity of the people of God.

The Church has purpose.	One aspect of the purpose of the Church is to partake of the Bread of Life so we can be changed to be more like Jesus and to take Jesus to the world.
Jesus Christ is the builder of the Church.	Jesus is the Bread of Life, and the Church grows as it partakes of the Word.
The Local Church is a defined body of believers.	Each loaf on the Table was a well-defined loaf of bread.
The Local Church is a gathering of believers identified with the name of Jesus Christ.	The 12 loaves were gathered together on the Table, and Jesus is the Bread of Life.

The Church walks in humility.	As partake of the Word of God, we grow in the knowledge of God and we realize how big God is and how small we are.
The Local Church is a spiritual family.	The 12 loaves represented the 12 tribes of Israel.
The Church teaches the Word of God.	Jesus was the Word made flesh and the Bread of Life.
The Church prays for the sick.	Jesus tells us in Matthew 15:26 that healing is the children's bread.
The Local Church has divine order.	The 12 loaves were placed on the Table in a specific way.
The Local Church functions in unity and agreement.	The 12 loaves were together in unity on the Table.
The local church is not yet perfect.	As the Church partakes of the Word of God, it is changed from Glory to Glory.
The Church is established in the faith (doctrine).	Eating the Bread of Life grounds the Church in the faith.
The leaders of the Church feed the Bread of Life to both young and old.	Jesus is the Bread of Life.
The Church acknowledges and celebrates Jesus' death, burial and resurrection by taking communion.	1 Corinthians 11:23b–24 "… the Lord Jesus on the same night in which He was betrayed took bread; and when He had given thanks, He broke it and said, 'Take, eat; this is My body which is broken for you; do this in remembrance of Me.'" Also Matthew 26:26-28.
The Church carries the Word everywhere they go.	As the Church partakes of the Bread of Life the Church carries God's Word with them everywhere they go.
The Church joins in voluntary fellowship with other local Churches.	The 12 loaves are arranged closely together on the Table.

ALTAR OF INCENSE
Jesus our Intercessor

The following traits are grouped here because the Altar of Incense represents worship and prayer ascending to the throne of God.

The Church has purpose.	One aspect of the purpose of the Church is to pray to and to worship our awesome God. "But you are a chosen generation, a royal priesthood, a holy nation, His own special people, that you may proclaim the praises of Him who called you out of darkness into His marvelous light." 1 Peter 2:9
Fellowship in faith and prayer is in the local Church.	Incense represents praise and prayer.
Singing is a part of Church worship.	One of the many forms of worship is singing.
In the midst of trials and tribulation the Church has peace.	We know that Jesus is interceding for us continually.
The Church is given to much prayer.	Incense was offered daily.
The Church is a House of Prayer for all the World.	Incense represents prayer, and the fragrance of incense flows out to the whole world.
The Church makes disciples.	Praise and prayer are important parts of a disciple's life.
Christians do not live unto themselves but unto Him.	Praise and worship keeps the focus on Jesus.
Ministry is sent out from the Church.	Incense flows out of the Tabernacle to the whole world.

ARK OF THE COVENANT
Jesus - fully God and fully man

The following traits are grouped here because the Ark of the Covenant represents God's provision, authority, and discipline.

The Church has purpose.	One aspect of the purpose of the Church is to be just like Jesus. Ephesians 4:13
The Church represents the authority of Christ on earth.	Aaron's rod represents God's delegated authority.
The local church exercises discipline when needed.	Aaron's rod also speaks of discipline.
God's authority channels through the local church.	Aaron's rod represents God's delegated authority.
The Church casts out demons in the name of Jesus.	Aaron's rod represents God's delegated authority.
The Church has individuals ordained in positions of authority to exercise leadership, discipline and oversight. These overseers are set in place by God, and it is their job to shepherd (with all that that means) the Church.	Aaron's rod represents God's delegated authority.

MERCY SEAT
Jesus the Presence of God
Jesus the Glory of God

The following traits are grouped here because the Mercy Seat represents the presence of God and His great mercy that is new every morning.

The Church has purpose.	One aspect of the purpose of the Church is to live in the presence of the Lord and the Mercy Seat represents His presence.
The message of the Church is Jesus Christ crucified, buried, raised from the dead, ascended into heaven, and living in His Church.	Salvation rests upon the mercy of God, so the message of the Church begins at the Brazen Altar and concludes at the Mercy Seat.
God hears and responds to the prayers and needs of the Church.	God said, "I will meet with you there." God meets us above the Mercy Seat. There He hears our prayers.
The Church lives in the love of God.	At the Mercy Seat we are in God's presence and to be in God's presence is to be immersed in His love.
Believers love Jesus more than anything else.	At the Mercy Seat we are in God's presence and in His presence everything else fades.

It has been said, "The Old Testament is the New Testament concealed: the New Testament is the Old Testament revealed." This correlation is very applicable to the Tabernacle that Moses built and the Church that Jesus is building.

As you think back over these chapters on the Tabernacle of Moses, I trust you see the connection to Jesus and His Church. The Tabernacle and the journey from the entry gate to the Holy of Holies is a wonderful outline that depicts the Christian's journey from sinner to full maturity.

Do you seem to be stuck at a particular place in your Christian walk?

What are some ways you can strive for breakthrough so you can help others grow in God?

Jesus is symbolized in each piece – explain changes we should expect in our lives as we encounter each piece of furniture in our Christian growth.
Gate –

Brazen Altar –

Brazen Laver –

Lampstand –

Table of Showbread –

Altar of Incense –

Ark of the Covenant –

Mercy Seat –

PART III

THE MISSION PREPARING THE CHURCH

THE WHOLE COUNSEL OF GOD
"You've got to be very careful if you don't know where you're going, because you might not get there." Yogi Berra

Throughout most of our Christian lives we have been taught that God's plan on earth is to bring unbelievers to salvation so that they will go to heaven. According to most preachers, the greatest thing we can do while we live on this earth is to bring lost souls to Christ. Now, I do not want to appear to be belittling the Gospel of Salvation. Jesus died for the sins of the world! And the message of the love of God that brings salvation through the blood of Jesus is the greatest message we can receive while we are still sinners. However, Paul speaking to the elders in Ephesus said: "Therefore I testify to you this day that I am innocent of the blood of all, for I did not shrink from declaring to you the whole counsel of God." (Acts 20:26-27 ESV) Paul was in Ephesus for more than three years declaring that whole counsel. There is a counsel of God that begins with salvation but includes so much more before we are finished with God's mission for each believer and for the Church as a whole here on earth.

Again I want to stress that the importance of the Gospel of Salvation cannot be overstated. In the natural, until a baby is born, there is nothing more important than that. There is no growth, there is no purpose, there is no destiny for a child until it comes to birth. But birth is not the end of the journey; natural birth is just the beginning of a lifetime of purpose and destiny as that child enters life to grow into a mature adult. Likewise in the Spirit, until we are born again there is no greater message than that of salvation. After new birth, however, the whole counsel of God must be added to the Gospel of Salvation. Peter expresses this concept in 2 Peter 1:5–7, "... giving all diligence, add to your faith virtue, to virtue knowledge, to knowledge self-control, to self-control perseverance, to perseverance godliness, to godliness brotherly kindness, and to brotherly kindness love." Everything begins with salvation (faith in Christ Jesus) but salvation is not the whole message. The Gospel of Salvation has been preached by the Church for many centuries so it is not the emphasis in this book. In this book we are endeavoring to look into the whole counsel of God.

If the main goal of God for His people is greater than going heaven, what is it? In Parts 3 & 4 of this book I want to focus on more of the whole counsel of God as expressed especially in the New Testament. It is beyond the ability of any one book or one writer to express the Mission of the Church as expressed in the whole counsel of God. I would love to have been present as Paul preached to the Ephesians the whole counsel of God. Many powerful books have been written that help to open up our understanding of God's purposes. "The Spiritual Man" by Watchman Nee, "Unto Full Stature" and "The Ultimate Intention" by DeVern Fromke, "The Purpose Driven Life" by Rick Warren, "Just Like Jesus" by Max Lucado along with multiple titles by Bill Johnson and Randy Clark and many other precious men and women of God are worth taking the time to read. In the following pages you will find what I believe to be some of the central aspects of the whole counsel of God that helps the Church fulfill its Mission.

With any mission there is a time of equipping and then the execution of the mission itself. Jesus told His disciples in John 20:21b–22, "'Peace to you! As the Father has sent Me, I also send you.' And when He had said this, He breathed on them, and said to them, 'Receive the Holy Spirit.'" Jesus had been equipping His disciples for three and one-half years and He gave them the Holy Spirit as the capstone of their preparation. Then in Acts 2:1-4 we see this Receiving of the Holy Spirit reach its fulfillment in what we speak of as the baptism of the Holy Spirit.

In this next section we will be dealing especially with the equipping of the Saints. Ephesians 4:11–12, "And He Himself gave some to be apostles, some prophets, some evangelists, and some pastors and teachers, for the equipping of the saints for the work of ministry, for the edifying of the body of Christ...."

In what areas do you feel like you need to be equipped?

How does limiting the entire mission of the church to salvation affect the Christian walk?

How does knowing God equips you to do His work give you confidence to press on to greater things in Him?

EQUIPPED - THE ETERNAL GODHEAD
(FATHER, SON AND HOLY SPIRIT)
OUR DIVINE ENABLER

As we consider the mission of the Church, one of the most important aspects is the truth expressed in Philippians 2:13, "for it is God who works in you both to will and to do for His good pleasure." When we look into the Word of God, we see just how completely God has made it possible for His Church to do all He expects them to do. In today's society, the word enabler has a negative connotation. An enabler is someone who encourages or enables negative or self-destructive behavior in another. However, the definition of that word is much broader. An enabler is a person or thing that makes something possible. With that definition in mind, let's look at what God has done to enable you to complete your mission as a part of His Church.

God's Word clearly declares that Jesus died on the cross to forgive us our sins. In 1 Corinthians 15:3 we read,

> *Jesus died to wipe the record of our sins out of our lives and out of the Book of Life!*

"For I delivered to you first of all that which I also received: that Christ died for our sins according to the Scriptures..." Jesus paid the penalty for our sin. We know what that penalty is from both the Old and New Testaments. In Genesis 2:17, "but of the tree of the knowledge of good and evil you shall not eat, for in the day that you eat of it you shall surely die." The penalty of sin is death. In Romans 6:23, "For the wages of sin is death, but the gift of God is eternal life in Christ Jesus our Lord." Again the penalty of sin is death. Jesus died to forgive us our sins so we don't have to die in our sins. His death on the cross paid the price for our sins and opened the door to everlasting life. But His death did so much more than that. Jesus died to wipe the record of those sins out of our lives and out of the Book of Life.

Psalm 32:1-2 Blessed is he whose transgression is forgiven, Whose sin is covered. (The best that could be done under the Old Covenant was that sins were covered from year to year.) Blessed is the man to whom the LORD does not impute iniquity, And in whose spirit there is no deceit.

Quoting Psalms 32:1-2, Paul writes in Romans 4:6-8, "just as David also describes the blessedness of the man to whom God imputes righteousness apart from works: Blessed are those whose lawless deeds are forgiven, And whose sins are covered; Blessed is the man to whom the LORD shall not <u>impute</u> sin."

The same Greek word for impute is translated as reckon in Romans 6:11. "Likewise you also, <u>reckon</u> yourselves to be dead indeed to sin, but alive to God in Christ Jesus our Lord."

This word translated as IMPUTE and RECKON is Strong's: 3049 [logizomai] and it means: to reckon, count, to make an account of; metaph. to pass to one's account, to impute.

God will not pass to our account the sins of our past. They are gone!

Again from Strong's: *"Additional Information: This word deals with reality. If I logizomai or reckon that my bank account has $25 in it, then it has $25 in it. If I reckon it has $0 in it, it has $0 in it." This word refers to facts not suppositions.*

So what we read here is that God will not pass to our account the sins of our past. They are gone!

We see a prophetic view of the absence of our sins in Psalm 103:12, "As far as the east is from the west, So far has He removed our transgressions from us." An interesting lesson in geography that is important here is that if God had said as far as the north is from the south that would have been a specific distance, at the farthest it would be one half of the circumference of the earth. But what God said as far as the east is from the west. You can never go so far west that you get to the east spot. As far as the east is from the west is always farther away from where you are. You cannot get there from here.   And then in Micah 7:19 (NIV), "You will again have compassion on us; you will tread our sins underfoot and hurl all our iniquities into the depths of the sea."

As Christians we must keep the truth close to our hearts that at salvation all things change. The Apostle Paul makes this very clear in 2 Corinthians 5:17, "Therefore, if anyone is in Christ, he is a new (Strong's: 2537 kainos: unused, unworn; also, of a new kind) creation; old things have passed away; behold, all things have become new." At salvation, we are not just changing who we serve (the devil or God) we go through a complete transformation from the old to the new.

God sees us as not just forgiven but also cleansed, changed into something new. And there is more. In Hebrews 9:14 (KJV) we read, "how much more shall the blood of Christ, who through the eternal Spirit offered Himself without spot to God, purge your <u>conscience</u> from dead works to serve the living God?" God has made it possible, through the sacrifice of His Son, for us to live life without shame.

> *God has made it possible, through the sacrifice of His Son, for us to live life without shame.*

Interestingly enough, the word conscience, as it is used here, should be looked at in a different way than we normally think of it. In Strong's: it is 4893 [suneidesis] translated as conscience 32 times. Its primary meaning is not our conscience but "the consciousness of anything." It is from the Greek word Strong's: (4894) [suneido] which means "to know in one's mind or with one's self, to be conscience of."

The thought here is more to be aware of than the thing we call our conscience. Looking at this Scripture with that in mind; we could translate Hebrews 9:14 as, "how much more shall the blood of Christ, who through the eternal Spirit offered Himself without spot to God, end our awareness of dead works [our sins] so that we can freely serve the living God?" How often does the "accuser of our brethren" (Revelation 12:10) bring up the sins of our past to convince us that we are so awful that we could never be used by God to do anything? God has wiped the heavenly record of our sins clean so that they will not be a hindrance to us as we press on into all the fullness of God! The sins of our past are not dead weights around our ankles to slow us down or drag us under. Our sins have been erased. Quit tormenting yourself about them! Paul tells us what things we are to think about. "Finally, brethren, whatsoever things are true, whatsoever things are honest, whatsoever things are just, whatsoever things are pure, whatsoever things are lovely, whatsoever things are of good report; if there be any virtue, and if there be any praise, think on these things." (Philippians 4:8 KJV)

Years ago I heard someone give this example: "When you pray, if you make reference to your past sins, God goes to His Book of Life and looks up your name. As He reads down He sees on page after page of your life 'washed in the blood of Jesus.' He would then say to you: 'I'm not sure what you're talking about, I don't see any mention of sin here.'" God not only forgives us the penalty of sin, He removes the stain of sin from our lives and from our conscience thought. Remember, satan is the accuser of the brethren, not God.

> *God has wiped the heavenly record of our sins clean so that they will not be a hindrance to us as we press on into all the fullness of God!*

Jesus' death on the cross was so powerful that the writer of Hebrews declares in chapter 10 verses 14–17 "For by one offering He has <u>perfected forever</u> those who are being sanctified. But the Holy Spirit also witnesses to us; for after He had said before, This is the covenant that I will make with them after those days,' says the LORD: 'I will put My laws into their hearts, and in their minds I will write them,' then He adds, 'Their sins and their lawless deeds I will remember no more.'" It's not that God can't remember our past sins, it is that He chooses to not remember them.

This word PERFECTED is the Greek word in Strong's: 5048 [teleioo]. It means to make perfect, complete; to carry through completely, to accomplish, finish, bring to an end; to add what is yet wanting in order to render a thing full; bring to a close or fulfilment by event.

The word FOREVER is Strong's: 1336 [dienekes]; and it is defined as: continuously, continuous.

The Message Bible translates Hebrews 10:14–17 in the following way: "It was a perfect sacrifice by a perfect person to perfect some very imperfect people. By that single offering, he did everything that needed to be done for everyone who takes part in the purifying process. The Holy Spirit confirms this: This new plan I'm making with Israel isn't going to be written on paper, isn't going to be chiseled in stone; this time 'I'm writing out the plan in them, carving it on the lining of their hearts.' He concludes, I'll forever wipe the slate clean of their sins." What a powerful declaration by Almighty God!

We are not supposed to look back at our old life, especially the sins of that old life. Luke 9:62 tells us "... No one, having put his hand to the plow, and looking back, is fit for the kingdom of God." So what do we do? "If then you were raised with Christ, seek those things which are above, where Christ is, sitting at the right hand of God. Set your mind on things above, not on things on the earth." (Colossians 3:1–2) We must deliberately refuse to look back and instead turn our eyes toward Jesus; the beginning and the end of our faith! Jesus removed the weight of our sin from our lives on the cross. By the removal of the weight and the guilt of the sin that caused that weight, Jesus enables us to start a new life free from all the entanglements of all our past sins.

What a glorious gift the Father has given us in the sacrifice of His son for our sins! It is not enough that our past sins are washed away by the Blood of Jesus; there is more!

As we press on in our walk with the Lord, His blood continues to wipe our sins away. The Apostle John, writing to those who were already believers states that, "if we walk in the light as He is in the light, we have fellowship with one another, and the blood of Jesus Christ His Son cleanses us from all sin. If we say that we have no sin, we deceive ourselves, and the truth is not in us. If we confess our sins, He is faithful and just to forgive us our sins and to cleanse us from all unrighteousness. If we say that we have not sinned, we make Him a liar, and His word is not in us." (1 John 1:7–10) This encouragement is not to unbelievers but to those who "walk in the light." Also, James in his letter to an existing church asked them the question. "Is anyone among you sick?" And then James gave them this advice. "Let him call for the elders of the church, and let them pray over him, anointing him with oil in the name of the Lord. And the prayer of faith will save the sick, and the Lord will raise him up. And if he has committed sins, he will be forgiven." (James 5:14–15) Forgiveness is the on-going cleansing of sin from our lives as we keep our relationship with Him strong and vital. When the accuser of the brethren lost the battle to keep me in defeat through throwing my past sins at me, he shifted to throwing my present sins at me. Jesus has taken care of them all by His Blood shed on the cross! Yes, when we stumble we need to ask God's forgiveness and forgiveness from the one we sinned against, but God's promise to us is that He is "faithful and just to forgive us our sins and to cleanse us from all unrighteousness." (1 John 1:9)

So the sin issue, past and present, is taken care of through the Blood of Jesus. As believers, walking in right relationship with God, we are cleansed of all sin and unrighteousness and the lies of satan throwing our past mistakes at us are nothing but lies. We must not let our enemy short-circuit our purpose in God by his empty lies. Jesus didn't stop with clearing away all the guilt and shame. Jesus didn't just take away hindrances to a successful life in Him, His indwelling presence enables us to live a successful life in Him.

> *The sin issue is taken care of through the Blood of Jesus.*

Jesus not only gave His life **for** us, He also gave His life **to** us! Jesus has enabled us to fulfill the destiny He has planned for us through the life He gives us. Jesus knew that we could not do this alone so He designed things, in His eternal purposes, so we wouldn't have to. Paul writes "... the commission God gave me to present to you the word of God in its fullness—the mystery that has been kept hidden for ages and generations, but is now disclosed to the saints. To them God has chosen to make known among the Gentiles the glorious riches of this mystery, which is Christ in you, the hope of glory." (Colossians 1:25–27 NIV) The hope of the glory of God being revealed to this world through His people is not only contingent upon us being in Christ but also on Christ being in His people.

God, the creator of the Universe, has chosen to live in His people. "Before long, the world will not see me anymore, but you will see me. Because I live, you also will live. On that day you will realize that I am in my Father, and you are in me, and I am in you." (John 14:19-20 NIV) "Jesus answered and said to him, "If anyone loves Me, he will keep My word; and My Father will love him, and We will come to him and make Our home with him." (John 14:23) Why the extreme emphasis on God living in believers? Because God's indwelling presence enables believers to draw on His life and to live a new creation life, a life free from sin, every day.

> *God's indwelling presence enables believers to draw on His life and to live a new creation life, a life free from sin, every day.*

Remember 2 Corinthians 5:17, "Therefore, if anyone is in Christ, he is a new creation; old things have passed away; behold, all things have become new."

We are literally different than we once were. "I have been crucified with Christ. It is no longer I who live, but Christ who lives in me. And the life I now live in the flesh I live by faith in the Son of God, who loved me and gave himself for me." (Galatians 2:20 ESV)

Philippians 1:6, "being confident of this very thing, that He who has begun a good work in you will complete it until the day of Jesus Christ; ...." The onus is on God. He gives us strength in the inner man. He gives us the strength to carry on. He is changing us from glory to glory. It is our part to believe God, to focus on Him, to press towards the high calling (Philippians 3:14). God Himself is the one who makes it happen.

Jeremiah 29:11 (NIV), "For I know the plans I have for you," declares the LORD, "plans to prosper you and not to harm you, plans to give you hope and a future."

How can we fail to fulfill God's purpose for our lives if the God who created the universe out of nothing is not only on our side but also lives in us to guide us and enable us in our life in Him? Is the problem our unwillingness to press into the things of God? What excuses do we have left after all that Jesus has done for us and in us? Remember, it is satan who is the accuser of the brethren not God. I read something recently that needs to be said here. "Satan knows our name but calls us by our sins. God knows our sins but calls us by our name." I would add to that the reminder that God knows our sins but has chosen to remember them no more.

WE HAVE THIS TREASURE

Now, lest we become big-headed, let us consider the following: "For God, who said, 'Let light shine out of darkness,' has shone in our hearts to give the light of the knowledge of the glory of God in the face of Jesus Christ. But we have this treasure in jars of clay, to show that the surpassing power belongs to God and not to us." (2 Corinthians 4:6-7 ESV)

First of all, what we have is called a treasure.

TREASURE from: On-line Webster's definition of treasure (as applies here):
- something of great worth or value also: a person esteemed as rare or precious
- a collection of precious things

We have been given the greatest treasure of all time in the form of not only the knowledge of the glory of God but in God Himself taking up residence within us. God is a treasure both rare and precious. This precious treasure (the triune God) has created us to be His dwelling place; to Him we are a treasure that He has restored unto Himself by the precious blood of His Son. (It is a hard-to-grasp truth that God loves His creation so much that He would rather die than live without us, until you remember that He calls us His children.) He is the treasure that has chosen to dwell in jars of clay. I love the King James Version here where it calls us earthen vessels. A potter can take clay from this earth and with a little water, work, and heat the potter can turn it into vessels fit for the Master's use.

God is the treasure; we are but earthen vessels and the purpose of this is to show that it is all about God!

Some important words used in 2 Corinthians 4:6-7:
The word surpassing (KJV excellency) is a very powerful Greek word. It speaks of beyond anything else.

SURPASSING from: Enhanced Strong's Lexicon: 5236 [huperbole]; metaphorically a throwing beyond; superiority, excellence, pre-eminence; beyond measure, exceedingly, preeminently.

The use of this word here is a resounding declaration that there is nothing greater than what follows; and that is power, power that is beyond all measure and that power belongs to God not us.

The word power is dunamis from which we get the word dynamite. Dynamite was the atomic bomb of its day. It was an extremely powerful explosive.

POWER from: Enhanced Strong's Lexicon: 411 [dunamis]; strength power, ability; an inherent power, power residing in a thing by virtue of its nature, or which a person or thing exerts and puts forth; power for performing miracles. Also moral power and excellence of soul; the power and influence which belong to riches and wealth; power and resources arising from numbers; power consisting in or resting upon armies, forces, hosts.

When you add the word huperbole to the word dunamis you get an expression of something that is beyond powerful; a power that nothing else can compare to. And this surpassing power belongs to God and not to us.

So, we could translate 2 Corinthians 4:7 as, "But we have this treasure in jars of clay, to show that this awesome power in us, this power to which no other power can compare, belongs to God and not to us."

God lives in us. His power resides

> *He who glories, let him glory in the Lord.*

with Him and so God's power is within us. But we must never forget that it is His power not ours. If His presence should ever leave us, His power would be gone! God has delegated to us authority over sickness, death, demonic spirits, and etc. but we ask God in the name of Jesus and all the glory belongs to God. We must never forget this truth.

Here are some final Scripture passages on this thought. The Apostle Paul says it so clearly: "But God has chosen the foolish things of the world to put to shame the wise, and God has chosen the weak things of the world to put to shame the things which are mighty; and the base things of the world and the things which are despised God has chosen, and the things which are not, to bring to nothing the things that are, that no flesh should glory in His presence. But of Him you are in Christ Jesus, who became for us wisdom from God—and righteousness and sanctification and redemption— that, as it is written, 'He who glories, let him glory in the Lord.'" (1 Corinthians 1:27-31) Under the Old Covenant, Israel could boast in their obedience to the letter of the Law. Paul says he could boast: "though I also might have confidence in the flesh. If anyone else thinks he may have confidence in the flesh, I more so: circumcised the eighth day, of the stock of Israel, of the tribe of Benjamin, a Hebrew of the Hebrews; concerning the law, a Pharisee; concerning zeal, persecuting the church; concerning the righteousness which is in the law, blameless." (Philippians 3:4–6) But the New Covenant is all about what Christ has done for us and in us and all the glory belongs to Him. "For by grace you have been saved through faith, and that not of yourselves; it is the gift of God, not of works, lest anyone should boast." (Ephesians 2:8–9)

As we ponder over the wonder of the awesome treasure we have, we must never forget that we have this treasure! In fact the greatest enabling that we have is because WE HAVE THIS TREASURE! God isn't just a treasure floating around and/or filling the universe. God, this God that in fact fills the universe, does in fact live in our hearts! So, let's study this aspect a little more.

How important are humans to God? We are the only part of all of God's creation that God took an active role in forming. "And the LORD God formed man of the dust of the ground, and breathed into his nostrils the breath of life; and man became a living soul." (Genesis 2:7 KJV) Everything else God spoke into existence. Humans are the only part of God's creation that God made to be like Him. "And God said, 'Let us make man in our image, after our likeness....' So God created man in his own image, in the image of God created he him; male and female created he them." (Genesis 1:26–27 KJV) And we are the only part of God's creation that He was willing to die for. God loves us so much that He would rather die than live without us.

With this in mind, in 2 Corinthians 4:7, "we have this treasure in jars of clay, to show that the surpassing power belongs to God and not to us", we need to look a little further into the specific Greek word used for treasure.

TREASURE- Enhanced Strong's Lexicon: 2344 [thesauros]. Not only does it refer to: the things laid up in a treasury, collected treasures. It also speaks to what holds the treasure: the place in which good and precious things are collected and laid up; a casket, coffer, or other receptacle, in which valuables are kept; treasury, storehouse, repository, magazine.

> *God loves us so much that He would rather die than live without us.*

A treasury is usually a very special place. Sometimes a treasury is very plain, sometimes a treasury is very beautiful (consider museums that house priceless works of art) but always treasuries are important to the owner of the treasure and are well guarded. Do not let the devil tell you that you aren't important to God. God has purposed to come into union with redeemed humanity. God has chosen to work in concert with His sons and daughters. Remember, it is "Christ in you, the hope of glory." (Colossians 1:27b)

DISCUSSION QUESTIONS FOR CHAPTER 8

Do you have a negative view of yourself? How does knowing God treasures you change that?

Describe the freedom that comes from life without the shame of sin.

What do you see as the mission of the Church or you yourself as a believer after Salvation?

Can you intentionally put yourself into situations where you are surrounded by unbelievers so you can share the Gospel?

How does the realization that Jesus Himself is the treasure in us, earthen vessels, affect you or show the surpassing power that belongs to God? How does it affect how you see other believers?

EQUIPPED
GOD'S GIFTINGS

God gives each of us supernatural help that matches the assignment He has for us. Some of this help comes as gifts from God that are in three distinct groupings; one group from God the Father, one group from Jesus Christ and one group from the Holy Spirit. This is not to limit the supernatural help from God to these groups, His help is unlimited, but these groups are special.

**Gifts (Enablings) from the Father: Motivational Gifts
(The make-up of our personality)**

God has given every one of us specific gifts that make up our personality. God personally gave us the right mix to help us fulfill our earthly mission (the purpose we have in Christ Jesus as born again Christians).

The following classifications come from Christian authors and are listed to point out that there are many ways to classify personality differences. Each of these authors have insight into the way our personalities differ, none of them are either right or wrong.

DIFFERENT WAYS OF CLASSIFYING PERSONALITIES

Classifications by C.P.Wagner
    people
    paper (ideas, plans)
    things

Classifications by Tim LaHaye
    choleric
    phlegmatic
    melancholic
    sanguine

Classifications by John Wimber
    radical --- pioneer
    progressive
    conservative
    traditional --- settler

Classifications by Ted Evans
    thinking
    feeling
    deciding
    relating
    speaking
    action
    creating
    directing
    observing
    helping
    nurturing

As our creator, God gives each individual person his/her own unique personality. The personality God gave us is motivated by God's great love for us, by our function in the Body of Christ and by our unique purpose on this earth. This unique personality was given to us in the womb and was activated for God's purposes when we were born again.

My preferred classifications come from Romans 12:6-8 (NIV), "We have different gifts, according to the grace given us. If a man's gift is prophesying, let him use it in proportion to his faith. If it is serving, let him serve; if it is teaching, let him teach; if it is encouraging, let him encourage; if it is contributing to the needs of others, let him give generously; if it is leadership, let him govern diligently; if it is showing mercy, let him do it cheerfully."

Without taking the time to go through a whole seminar about our personalities, let's look briefly at the seven characteristics from Romans 12:6-8.

Prophesying (To keep from confusing this personality gift with the Ministry gift of prophecy, I like to use the term *Perceiving*.)
Serving
Teaching
Encouraging
Giving
Leading
Showing Mercy

Each person is born with a mix of one or two of these traits dominating their personality and the rest blending with differing levels of influence. These traits can be demonstrated in the following story:

A little girl at a church luncheon goes to get some dessert. As she gets it, she runs across the room and drops the bowl and it breaks, making a mess. Here are sample responses based on these traits.

"I think maybe you were too excited to get started eating that dessert, weren't you? When you run with something, you might end up spilling it. Maybe you should have waited for your mom to help you." (*Perceiver*)

"OK, don't worry, I'll clean it up for you. You just sit right here, and I'll get you another one." (*Server*)

"Do you know why this happened? When you carry a bowl of something you need to hold it securely with two hands. Like this. Then you walk very slowly and carefully. Understand?" (*Teacher*)

"Hey, that's all right. Everybody has accidents. Don't you worry, just be careful of the broken glass and run back to the kitchen for another bowl." (*Encourager*)

"Here, I have a tissue (to dry her tears). Now, let's go get another bowl." or "Here you can have mine, I'll get another one." (*Giver*)

"Mary, we have a mess here, (i.e. come take care of it, please). Judy, could you see to the little girl? I'm going to suggest to the group that the children go through the line with their parents. (*Leader*)

"Are you OK? You didn't hurt yourself, did you? I know how you feel. Once I did something like this. But you know what? No one's upset with you. As long as you're all right, everything is OK." (*Mercy*)

> **Remember, "we" have the mind of Christ not "I".**

Which of these responses is the correct one? All of them are correct, depending on your point of view. Are any of these answers wrong? No! I learned from this study how important different viewpoints are in the Body of Christ. As a young elder, I felt it was my job to convince others that my point of view was the best (or only correct) point of view. Now I understand that different points of view are not only to be tolerated but to be valued. As we value each person's unique gifting and thus unique viewpoint we can blend them together to get a more Christ-like response to every situation that we face. Remember, we have the mind of Christ not I. (1 Corinthians 2:16)

There is an interesting story that illustrates this important truth. This story comes from my childhood and is called "The Blind Men and the Elephant" by James Baldwin. You might remember it too, if not here it is:

"There were once six blind men who stood by the road-side every day, and begged from the people who passed. They had often heard of elephants, but they had never seen one; for, being blind, how could they?

It so happened one morning that an elephant was driven down the road where they stood. When they were told that the great beast was before them, they asked the driver to let him stop so that they might see him.

Of course they could not see him with their eyes; but they thought that by touching him they could learn just what kind of animal he was.

The first one happened to put his hand on the elephant's side. "Well, well!" he said, "now I know all about this beast. He is exactly like a wall."

The second felt only of the elephant's tusk. "My brother," he said, "you are mistaken. He is not at all like a wall. He is round and smooth and sharp. He is more like a spear than anything else."

The third happened to take hold of the elephant's trunk. "Both of you are wrong," he said. "Anybody who knows anything can see that this elephant is like a snake."

The fourth reached out his arms, and grasped one of the elephant's legs. "Oh, how blind you are!" he said. "It is very plain to me that he is round and tall like a tree."

The fifth was a very tall man, and he chanced to take hold of the elephant's ear. "The blindest man ought to know that this beast is not like any of the things that you name," he said. "He is exactly like a huge fan."

The sixth was very blind indeed, and it was some time before he could find the elephant at all. At last he seized the animal's tail. "O foolish fellows!" he cried. "You surely have lost your senses. This elephant is not like a wall, or a spear, or a snake, or a tree; neither is he like a fan. But any man with a particle of sense can see that he is exactly like a rope."

Then the elephant moved on, and the six blind men sat by the roadside all day, and quarreled about him. Each believed that he knew just how the animal looked; and each called the others hard names because they did not agree with him. People who have eyes sometimes act as foolishly."

Again, we see that they were all correct, but only in part. They needed each other to get the full picture.

An important note: Your personality, when you come to Christ, is not the one God gave you in your mother's womb. That personality has been warped and perverted by a fallen creation, but as you yield your life to the Holy Spirit, it is renewed and brought back to God's original intent. As a pastor, one of the things that frustrates me is when I counsel someone about a bad attitude and their response is: "Well that's just the way God made me." God did NOT make you that way; life might have made you that way, but not God.

> *Your personality, when you come to Christ, is not the one God gave you in your mother's womb.*

This is a good place to bring up Galatians 5:22–23, "But the fruit of the Spirit is love, joy, peace, longsuffering, kindness, goodness, faithfulness, gentleness, self-control. Against such there is no law." The Fruit of the Spirit must affect our personalities. The Fruit of the Spirit is something that we don't even have until after salvation and the fruit doesn't come into our lives as mature fruit; it comes into our lives as seed. Just as natural fruit begins as a seed and grows to maturity, so the fruit of the Spirit comes into our lives as seeds that we must nourish and grow. We must cultivate it and help it grow to maturity in our individual new-creation life.

Because we live in a fallen world, each of these personality types has both strengths and weaknesses. To get a full understanding of this approach you can get workbooks from Heart to Heart International Ministries. The specific one I have worked with is "Discover Your God Given Gifts" by Don and Katie Fortune. Their web page is heart2heart.org.

Gifts (Enablings) from the Son: Ministerial Gifts

Jesus Christ Himself has given some gifts to His Church. These gifts are given to men and women anointed by the Holy Spirit and given by Christ to the Church to help the Church fulfill its mission here on the earth.

These gifts are listed in Ephesians 4:11-13, "And He Himself gave some to be apostles, some prophets, some evangelists, and some pastors and **teachers**, for the equipping of the saints for the work of ministry, for the edifying of the body of Christ, till we all come to the unity of the faith and of the knowledge of the Son of God, to a perfect man, to the measure of the stature of the fullness of Christ;"

Some call these gifted ministries and some speak of those who function in the office of an apostle, prophet, etc. These gifts work with the motivational gifts. Where would the Church be without these God-called men and women functioning in their gifts equipping and edifying the body of Christ? We need them, all of them, to complete our mission. Most of us have a basic understanding of the ministries of pastor, teacher and evangelist. We will study the gifts of Apostle and Prophet later on in this book.

Gifts from the Holy Spirit: Manifestation Gifts

These gifts, given by the Holy Spirit, are not given until after salvation. These are called by some the power gifts and as such I believe are given at the time a believer is baptized in the Holy Spirit or later. The reasoning for this comes from Luke 24:49, "Behold, I send the Promise of My Father upon you; but tarry in the city of Jerusalem until you are endued with power from on high." Jesus is instructing His followers about the next step in their life in Him and we see it fulfilled in Acts 2:1–4, "When the Day of Pentecost had fully come, they were all with one accord in one place. And suddenly there came a sound from heaven, as of a rushing mighty wind, and it filled the whole house where they were sitting. Then there appeared to them divided tongues, as of fire, and one sat upon each of them. And they were all filled with the Holy Spirit and began to speak with other tongues, as the Spirit gave them utterance."

1 Timothy 4:14, "Do not neglect the gift that is in you, which was given to you by prophecy with the laying on of the hands of the eldership." 2 Timothy 1:6, "Therefore I remind you to stir up the

gift of God which is in you through the laying on of my hands." These Scriptures imply that gifts can be imparted by, at minimum, the eldership and Apostles.

Now, let us look at specific gifts. 1 Corinthians 12:1, "Now concerning spiritual gifts, brethren, I do not want you to be ignorant: 4 There are diversities of gifts, but the same Spirit. 11 But one and the same Spirit works all these things, distributing to each one individually as He wills."

1 Corinthians 12:7-10, "But the manifestation of the Spirit is given to each one for the profit of all: for to one is given the word of wisdom through the Spirit, to another the word of knowledge through the same Spirit, to another faith by the same Spirit, to another gifts of healings by the same Spirit, to another the working of miracles, to another prophecy, to another discerning of spirits, to another different kinds of tongues, to another the interpretation of tongues."

Paul, under the inspiration of the Holy Spirit, declared these gifts to be important for the Church.
1 Corinthians 14:39 "Therefore, brethren, desire earnestly to prophesy."
1 Corinthians 14:1 "... and desire spiritual gifts, but especially that you may prophesy."
1 Thessalonians 5:19-20 "Do not quench the Spirit, do not despise prophecies."

Much has been said and written about Spiritual gifts so I will not repeat it. I just want to encourage you to seek out and to grow in the gifts God has entrusted to you. These tools aren't trophies to be put on a shelf and admired; they are to be used here on this earth to advance the Kingdom of God both in peoples' lives and in this world. These gifts are tools given by God to us for us to use now. You won't need them in heaven.

It is important to point out that none of the miracles Jesus did were done to draw attention to Himself. In fact, most of the time He instructed those who were healed to not tell anyone. His miracles were all done out of His compassion for people and to fulfill His purpose of destroying the works of the devil. In the same way, gifts given by God at salvation are not to advance our position or to feed our ego or to make us look more Spiritual to others. Our gifts must put the focus on God and be evidence of God's love in action.

DISCUSSION QUESTIONS FOR CHAPTER 9

How can you learn more about God's gifts in your life?

How can you value the personalities of your family, Church family, and friends?

What 1, 2 or 3 personality types can you see in yourself?

EQUIPPED

A SPIRITUAL FAMILY

Jesus grew up in the natural family of Joseph and Mary together with His brothers and sisters but He implied a different kind of family as well. "But He answered and said to the one who told Him, 'Who is My mother and who are My brothers?' And He stretched out His hand toward His disciples and said, 'Here are My mother and My brothers! For whoever does the will of My Father in heaven is My brother and sister and mother.'" (Matthew 12:48–50) God's family, those who are truly born again, is much bigger than Jesus' natural mother, and siblings.

In Ephesians 2:19 the Apostle Paul, writing to believers, expresses this new kind of family this way. "Now, therefore, you are no longer strangers and foreigners, but fellow citizens with the saints and members of the <u>household</u> of God," So, not only do we become citizens of God's kingdom, we also become a part of God's <u>household</u>, His family.

HOUSEHOLD: Enhanced Strong's Lexicon: 3609 [oikeios]; belonging to a house or family, domestic, intimate, related by blood, kindred; belonging, devoted to, adherents of a thing.

Ephesians 3:14–15, For this reason I bow my knees to the Father of our Lord Jesus Christ, from whom the whole <u>family</u> in heaven and earth is named,

FAMILY: Enhanced Strong's Lexicon: 3965 [patria]; lineage running back to some progenitor, ancestry; a race or tribe; all those who in a given people lay claim to a common origin.

Ephesians 3:14-15 (above) could be telling that all of mankind came from Adam and Eve, but since it includes the idea of heaven and earth together it must be talking about those born again and whether in heaven or on earth they are all a part of the family of God. I believe that on the earth a Godly family is the closest thing to what life will be like in Heaven. I know that very few people are privileged to grow up in a Godly family, but if you can imagine what the best family on earth would be like, that and more is what relationships will be like in Heaven. There Jesus will not only be known as our Savior but also our elder brother (Hebrews 2:11).

> *Love is the true cornerstone of family.*

The foundation of a family and the continued functioning as a family must be centered in love. True love is a motivator as well as an enabler. Paul instructs us in Colossians 3:19, "Husbands, love your wives and do not be bitter toward them." And in Titus 2:4, "... admonish the young women to love their husbands, to love their children...." Many times I have counselled the new husband in a blended family to establish a love relationship with his new children before he shoulders the responsibility of disciplining them. This principle is reflected in both the Old and New Testaments.

Proverbs 3:11–12, My son, do not despise the chastening of the LORD, Nor detest His correction; For whom the LORD <u>loves</u> He corrects, Just as a father the son in whom he delights.

Revelation 3:19a, As many as I <u>love</u>, I rebuke and chasten.

Did you notice that love came first?! Love is the true cornerstone of family. During the time I was writing this book God made me aware of this in a very unique way.

I was driving from Kansas City to Springfield. On that drive I was listening to some of my favorite songs from the Jesus People era. I was enjoying not only the songs but the journey down memory lane. The song "How Lovely Is Thy Dwelling Place" by Ted Sandquist began to play. When the song got to the line "and the highway to your city runs through my heart," the presence of God filled the car and flooded my being. As I basked in the presence of God, I realized that His presence didn't come with the songs I was listening to; it came with this specific line. I wrestled in my mind trying to understand what God was saying to me. I went so far as to ask a number of people to pray and see what God was wanting me to understand about that line but I didn't get any answers. Then, one day as I was walking through our church building, the Lord dropped this into my mind: "The way to the city of God runs through your heart not through your mind." The heart is the seat of our emotions and the greatest emotion in our heart is love.

> **True love is proactive!**

Our salvation, our life in God, our growth in God, reaching our destiny in God is not mainly about our intellectual understanding of the Scripture, it is about our heart. Romans 10:10 tells us, "For with the heart one believes unto righteousness, and with the mouth confession is made unto salvation." John 3:16 declares, "For God so loved the world that He gave His only begotten Son, that whoever believes in Him should not perish but have everlasting life." Old Testament Scriptures shout of God's love for us. In the book of the Song of Solomon 1:2b, the bride speaking to the bridegroom declares, "For your love is better than wine." and the bridegroom says to his bride, 1:7 "Tell me, O you whom I love...."

True love is a two-way street. We love God but our love is a response to Him having loved us first. The psalmist speaks of our love/devotion toward God in Psalm 42:1, "As the deer pants for the water brooks, So pants my soul for You, O God." Song of Solomon says this of our love for God in chapter 5 verse 8, "I charge you, O daughters of Jerusalem, If you find my beloved, That you tell him I am lovesick!" God is love and we were designed by Him to be recipients of and responders to His love.

Undoubtedly, sound doctrine is important. Jesus charged Peter three times in John 21:15-17, "feed my sheep," so it must be important! However, it is not as important as love. We will make all kinds of sacrifices to put a smile on the face of the one we love. In fact if you find yourself doing less out of your love for someone, a friend, your children, your spouse, or even God; you need to ask God to renew your love for that person or for Him. True love is proactive. No one had to tell God to sacrifice His Son for humanity. God gave His Son willingly because of His great love for us.

The word love shows up in the Bible more than three times as often as the word obey.

Along with sound doctrine, obedience is very important in our relationship with God. We are told in 1 Samuel 15:22, "to obey is better than sacrifice." Obedience is a very important part of our relationship with God. However, love is even more important in our relationship with God than obedience. The word love shows up in the Bible more than three times as often as the word obey. Obedience applies to relationships between people and kings, servants and masters, employees and employers, children and parents, etc. Obedience isn't applicable when we talk about relationships between friends, between adult children and parents, or between husbands and wives who truly love each other. We do for one another because we love each other. Our love is expressed through our words and actions.

I want to address the importance of relationships a little more. In Genesis 2:18-20 (TMB), "God said, 'It's not good for the Man to be alone; I'll make him a helper, a companion.'" God recognized Adam's need for relationship. "So God formed from the dirt of the ground all the animals of the field and all the birds of the air. He brought them to the Man to see what he would name them. Whatever the Man called each living creature, that was its name. The Man named the cattle, named the birds of the air, named the wild animals; but he didn't find a suitable companion." Adam was looking for a companion, not a pet. You can love your pet but not in the same way you love your spouse or your children. Why? Because humans are not the same as any animal in the whole world. God made man exclusively in His image and after His likeness. God breathed the breath of life into Adam and

> *Our love is expressed by our actions.*

Adam alone. Adam didn't understand it then but he was looking for someone who was flesh of his flesh and bone of his bone.

Continuing in Genesis 2:21-24 (NLT): "So the Lord God caused the man to fall into a deep sleep. While the man slept, the Lord God took out one of the man's ribs and closed up the opening. Then the Lord God made a woman from the rib, and he brought her to the man. 'At last!' the man exclaimed. 'This one is bone from my bone, and flesh from my flesh! She will be called "woman," because she was taken from "man." This explains why a man leaves his father and mother and is joined to his wife, and the two are united into one." (The Hebrew Interlinear using the Hebrew Text: Westminster Leningrad Codex shows something here that is not in any translation I have ever read. When Adam exclaimed "At last!" that's not exactly what he said. He exclaimed "This one!" not once, not twice but three times!) The text shows Adam's excitement! I don't think Adam wanted God to miss "this one!" This one was his choice. Flesh of his flesh and bone of his bone, for sure.

You cannot have a truly loving relationship with something that is not like you. God was acting on this fact when He said, "...Let Us make man in Our image, according to Our likeness...." (Genesis 1:26) We are told in 1 John 4:8, "He who does not love does not know God, for God is love." God had already created all the

> *God made man exclusively in His image and after His likeness.*

heavenly hosts and all the living things on the earth but to find someone He could really love He had to create one in His image and after His likeness. God knew that He was going to love mankind so much that He would rather die than live without them. That's why Jesus is called, "the Lamb slain from the foundation of the world." (Revelation 13:8b) Before man sinned, God knew that he would sin. So God, in His great love, prepared a solution for man's sin. He prepared a sacrifice, His only begotten Son, to die in our place for our sins so our relationship with God could be restored. No wonder Paul exclaims, "But God, who is rich in mercy, because of His great love with which He loved us, even when we were dead in trespasses, made us alive together with Christ (by grace you have been saved), and raised us up together, and made us sit together in the heavenly places in Christ Jesus, that in the ages to come He might show the exceeding riches of His grace in His kindness toward us in Christ Jesus." (Ephesians 2:4–7) Why? Because of His great love for us, "For we are members of His body, of His flesh and of His bones." (Ephesians 5:30)

Carl Sagan (1934-1996), a noted astronomer, once said: "The nitrogen in our DNA, the calcium in our teeth, the iron in our blood, the carbon in our apple pies were made in the interiors of collapsing stars. We are made of star stuff. (My emphasis.) I would like to acknowledge the truth of what he said but add to this astounding information the greater truth that according to the Word of God we are made of God Stuff! Selah! God made us "in His image and after His likeness" (Genesis 1:26) "of His flesh and of His bones" (Ephesians 5:30) so that not a weak watered-down version of His love might be bestowed upon His creation but that the fullness of His love might be poured out of His heart into His children.

> *Our heavenly Father wants a father-son relationship with His children.*

One more illustration of this truth is in the parable of The Prodigal Son.   A major aspect of this parable that sometimes gets overlooked speaks to us of relationships, both good and bad.

If you haven't read the parable recently, you might take time to read it now. Luke 11:15-32

As you examine this parable closely, you will see three different relationships described; the relationship of father to son, of son to father and servant to master. The problem here is that only one of the sons had a father-son relationship, the younger son. Even though he took his inheritance and left home, he called his father, Father and recognized himself as a son. Only sons have an inheritance, not servants. The elder son did not call his father, Father even once. Even in the Greek Interlinear it is missing. He also doesn't refer to his brother as Brother. The elder son talks to his father and calls his brother this son of yours. The younger son when he wants to come back and just be a servant still calls his father, Father. When the elder son is coming in from the field and hears the noise, he doesn't go to his father to find out what is going on, he goes to a servant. The elder brother describes his relationship with his father as that of a servant, "I have been serving you" but that was not the heart of the father. The father in this parable always refers to each of his sons as Son.

God, Who Jesus told us to call "Father", our heavenly Father, does not want to have a master-servant relationship with us, His children. Our heavenly Father clearly wants to have a father-son relationship. Remember, Jesus said that we must be born again. This Scripture directly addresses our relationship with God as Father. (See also Romans 8:15-16)

> *Obedience pleases God but doing the right thing out of a heart of love without His direct instructions brings Him delight.*

I want to add a little side note here that deals with us being motivated by love.

Did you know that you can bring delight to God? God gives us some tremendous insight into this concept in Jeremiah 9:23–24. "Thus says the LORD: 'Let not the wise man glory in his wisdom, Let not the mighty man glory in his might, Nor let the rich man glory in his riches; But let him who glories glory in this, That he understands and knows Me, That I am the LORD, exercising lovingkindness, judgment, and righteousness in the earth. For in these I delight,' says the LORD." Here God is not giving us a list of rules so we can obey Him. He is telling us the things that bring Him delight. Don't you think then that when out of our heart, because of our love for God, we exercise lovingkindness, when we work for just judgment and when we endeavor to be righteous in all we do, it brings God delight? Delight is not produced out of obedience; it is produced when we do something that pleases someone out of our love for them. Obedience pleases God but doing the right thing out of a heart of love without His direct instructions brings Him delight. Find a way to put a smile on God's face today!

DISCUSSION QUESTIONS FOR CHAPTER 10

Describe the difference in the relationships between master/ servant and father/son. How does this change/grow your relationship with God?

You are part of God's family. How does this affect your prayer life, your relationship, your ministry, your love for your Spiritual brothers and sisters?

What is the difference between obedience from obligation and doing the right thing as a result of love?

EQUIPPED
GROWING SPIRITUALLY

NEWBORNS TO MATURE SONS AND DAUGHTERS

We all start life as sinners. No matter how old we are in our natural life when we accept Jesus as our personal Savior we are babies in our Spiritual life. Jesus explained this to Nicodemus one night in John 3:3–6. "Jesus answered and said to him, 'Most assuredly, I say to you, unless one is born again, he cannot see the kingdom of God.' Nicodemus said to Him, 'How can a man be born when he is old? Can he enter a second time into his mother's womb and be born?' Jesus answered, 'Most assuredly, I say to you, unless one is born of water and the Spirit, he cannot enter the kingdom of God. That which is born of the flesh is flesh, and that which is born of the Spirit is spirit.'" What's the big deal about being born again? Can't we just explain what happens at salvation as conversion, or an enlightening, or a religious experience or in some other way? Why did Jesus use a phrase that had to do with childbirth? Let me explain it this way.

> **Because of your new birth you have a new nature.**

One time as a young adult I was complaining to God about how hard it was to live the Christian life. I had just heard some teaching on loving your enemy and losing your life for Christ's sake and sincerely wanted to change but it was so hard. As I was complaining, I said, "God, it's hard to live the way you want me to, it's like trying to push a chain, it just won't work." I stopped to take a breath and I clearly heard the voice of God speaking to my heart.

God: "Why do you think I said 'you must be born again'?"

Me: "I don't know."

God: "All living creatures are born with a distinctive nature and you, being born into this world as a sinner, had a sinful nature. However, you have been born again and have become a new creation, old things have passed away, all things have become new. Why do you think an elephant acts like an elephant, or a dog like a dog? Because it is their nature. No one expects an elephant to fly or a dog to climb trees. You acted like a sinner because you were one but you are not a sinner anymore. You are a child of God. Because of your new birth you have a new nature; you don't have to make yourself live the Christian life, you just need to let the new life that is in you come out rather than the habits you learned in your old life. It is hard to push a chain but it is very easy to pull one."

Wow, what a revelation! I was looking at things all wrong. I really wasn't who I used to be, I was a child of God with a different nature. I didn't have to try and be different, I really was different but I needed to learn what the differences were and how to let them change my thoughts and behavior.

The Apostle Peter confirms this in 1 Peter 1:23 where he states that we, "hav(e) been born again, not of corruptible seed but incorruptible, through the word of God which lives and abides forever...." This new life that we have within us comes from the incorruptible seed of the Spirit. The Apostle John, writing about those who come to Christ, says; "But as many as received Him, to them He gave the right to become children of God, to those who believe in His name: who were born, not of blood, nor of the will of the flesh, nor of the will of man, but of God." (John 1:12–13) If we are born of God, then He is our father and our nature comes from

If we are born of God, then He is our father and our nature comes from Him.

Him. Jesus taught us to pray, Our Father and Paul wrote, "For you did not receive a spirit that makes you a slave again to fear, but you received the Spirit of sonship. And by him we cry, 'Abba, Father'." (Romans 8:15 NIV) This Scripture also confirms this new Spiritual relationship.

The Apostle John pointed this out in John 1:11–12, "He came to His own, and His own did not receive Him. But as many as received Him, to them He gave the right to become children of God, to those who believe in His name".

CHILDREN - Vines – teknon: child, gives prominence to the fact of birth

So, teknon emphasizes the reality and importance of the relationship:
"Ye must be born again...." John 3:3
"Our Father which art in heaven...." Matthew 6:9
"I will be his God and he shall be My son...." Revelation 21:7

So, we come to the Lord by new birth, that speaks of starting our Spiritual life as a Spiritual baby. Peter points this out in 1 Peter 2:2 (NLT) "You must crave pure spiritual milk so that you can grow into the fullness of your salvation." No one, no matter how mature he is in the natural, is born into the family of God fully mature. We come into the family of God as infants but can grow rapidly or we can continue too long as infants. The Apostle Paul rebukes the Church at Corinth for not maturing. 1 Corinthians 3:1-2 (NLT) "Dear brothers and sisters, when I was with you I couldn't talk to you as I would to mature Christians. I had to talk as though you belonged to this world or as though you were infants in the Christian life. I had to feed you with milk and not with solid food, because you couldn't handle anything stronger. And you still aren't ready...."

The process of Spiritual development is explored in 2 Peter 1:5-7, "But also for this very reason, giving all diligence, add to your faith virtue, to virtue knowledge, to knowledge self-control, to self-control perseverance, to perseverance godliness, to godliness brotherly kindness, and to brotherly kindness love." Everything about our new life begins with our faith in Jesus Christ as our Savior but it doesn't end there. This theme continues in 2 Peter 3:17-18, "You therefore, beloved... beware lest you also fall from your own steadfastness, being led away with the error of the wicked; but grow in the grace and knowledge of our Lord and Savior Jesus Christ." And in Hebrews 6:1-3, "Therefore, leaving the discussion of the elementary principles of Christ, let us go on to perfection, not laying again the foundation of repentance from dead works and of faith toward God, of the doctrine of baptisms, of laying on of hands, of resurrection of the dead, and of eternal judgment. And this we will do if God permits." Our Spiritual growth is important enough to God that He reminds us of it again and again throughout the Scriptures.

In Galatians 4:1–2, Paul points out the parallel between being a child and a servant/slave. "Now I say that the heir, as long as he is a child, does not differ at all from a slave, though he is master of all, but is under guardians and stewards until the time appointed by the father." Even though we grow in our relationship with God, we will never stop being His child. We should also never stop identifying as His servant. Both the Apostle Paul and the Apostle James made it clear about their thoughts on this matter; "Paul, a servant of God, and an apostle of Jesus Christ." (Titus 1:1 KJV) and "James, a servant of God and of the Lord Jesus Christ...." (James 1:1 KJV) The Apostle Peter tells all of us to "Live as free men, but do not use your freedom as a cover-up for evil; live as servants of God." (1 Peter 2:16 NIV)

> *Everything about our new life begins with our faith in Jesus Christ as our Savior but it doesn't end there.*

As we grow in our relationship with God, we should always have the heart of a servant. Jesus taught, "You know that those who are considered rulers over the Gentiles lord it over them, and their great ones exercise authority over them. Yet it shall not be so among you; but whoever desires to become great among you shall be your servant. And whoever of you desires to be first shall be slave of all." (Mark 10:42b–44) Jesus pointed out the importance of having a servant's heart in John 13 when He washed His disciples' feet. Having a servant's heart is the foundation of who we are and all that we do as Christians.

As we progress in our relationship with God through Bible study, prayer, Christian fellowship, gathering together with fellow Christians in what we call Church services and more, we grow into a relationship as friends with Jesus and fellow Christians. Jesus told His disciples, "You are My friends if you do whatever I command you. No longer do I call you servants, for a servant does not know what his master is doing; but I have called you friends, for all things that I heard from My Father I have made known to you." (John 15:14-15)

Abraham had such a relationship with God that he was called God's friend. We read in James 2:23 (KJV), "And the Scripture was fulfilled which saith, Abraham believed God, and it was imputed

> *Having a servant's heart is the foundation of who we are and all that we do as Christians.*

unto him for righteousness: and he was called the Friend of God." A good child/servant relationship is based upon obedience to the commands of one's father/master. A good friendship is based upon having similar likes and dislikes, enjoying the same things; in other words, enjoying and wanting to be together. My wife, whom I love dearly, is also my best friend. I would rather spend time with her than anyone else I know.

Are you a friend of God like King David who declared, "I was glad when they said to me, 'Let us go into the house of the LORD.'" (Psalm 122:1) or do you have to be dragged to the Church? Do you love spending time with Him in the Word and in prayer or can you never seem to find the time for that? Is praise and worship a highlight of your day or do you get bored and restless during praise and worship and hope they will get on with the service? Have you grown into a friendship relationship with God or are you only a servant? A servant's heart is the right attitude but friendship is a better relationship; but it can get even better.

We are born a child/servant, we grow to be a friend, but our goal should be to be adopted or placed as God's own sons. We are not addressing the fact that Jesus is the "only begotten Son of God" (John:18). We are addressing the fact that repeatedly the followers of Jesus are addressed as His brothers, God's sons. We, His children, must address the reality of growing into the relationship and responsibility of mature sons and daughters of God.

After Jesus' death, burial and resurrection, He called His disciples His brothers. "Jesus said to her (Mary), '... go to My brethren and say to them, "I am ascending to My Father and your Father, and to My God and your God."'" (John 20:17) Here Jesus points out that He relates to us as brothers because we have the same Father that He does. This is mentioned and expanded upon by the Apostle Paul in Romans 8:28-29 where Paul writes, "And we know that all things work together for good to those who love God, to those who are the called according to His purpose. For whom He foreknew, He also predestined to be conformed to the image of His Son, that He might be the firstborn among many brethren." Here Paul points out that we become brothers to Jesus as we are being conformed to the image of Jesus.

But it isn't only Jesus calling us brothers, God calls us His sons. Sons and brothers share more than just common interests, they share the same DNA. They grow up in the same home they share the same values, the same vision, the same heart. The Apostle Paul shares in Romans 8:14, "For as many as are led by the Spirit of God, these are sons (huios) of God." We also read "He who overcomes shall inherit all things, and I will be his God and he shall be My son (huios)." (Revelation 21:7)

> *Have you grown into a friendship relationship with God or are you only a servant?*

In this final area of Christian growth, we need to examine some hard-to-define words that are used in the New Testament. Huios - a son versus teknon - a child or young son. In my research I came upon various ways to explain the differences between these words, some of them were very confusing, so I decided to go with Vine's New Testament

Dictionary. It seemed to differentiate between the words in the clearest manner.

From Vine's New Testament Dictionary we have:
Huios: "a son" primarily signifies the relation of offspring to parent. (see John 9:18-20; Gal 4:30) It is often used metaphorically of prominent moral attributes (as opposed to simply the birth of a male child "teknon").

Notes: (continuing with Vine's)
"(1) For the synonyms teknon and teknion see under CHILD. The difference between believers as 'children of God' and as 'sons of God' is brought out in Rom 8:14-21. The Spirit bears witness with their spirit that they are 'children of God,' and, as such, they are His heirs and joint-heirs with Christ. This stresses the fact of their spiritual birth (Rom 8:16-17). On the other hand, 'as many as are led by the Spirit of God, these are sons of God,' i.e., 'these and no other.' Their conduct gives evidence of the dignity of their relationship and their likeness to His character."

Examples of the use of huios in Matthew. In chapter 5:9, "Blessed are the peacemakers, For they shall be called sons (huios) of God." and in chapter 5:44–45a, "But I say to you, love your enemies, bless those who curse you, do good to those who hate you, and pray for those who spitefully use you and persecute you, that you may be sons (huios) of your Father in heaven...." Both of these Scriptures are clearly speaking of followers of Jesus and imply a significant maturity of those

> *We, His children, must address the reality of growing into the relationship and responsibility of mature sons and daughters of God.*

who would be called sons (huios) as compared to being a male child (teknon).

Some would argue that the Greek word huios is also used in the genealogies of Jesus to mean male child or male descendent, not a mature son. However, as in all writings, context is very important.

And then there is the word ADOPTION – Strongs: 5206 [huiothesia] from huios - a son, and thesis - a placing, akin to tithemi - to place. The word is used by the Apostle Paul only.

Quoting from Vines' New Testament Dictionary:
"In Rom 8:15, believers are said to have received "the Spirit of adoption," that is, the Holy Spirit who, given as the Firstfruits of all that is to be theirs, produces in them the realization of sonship and the attitude belonging to sons. In Gal 4:5 they are said to receive "the adoption of sons," i.e., sonship bestowed in distinction from a relationship consequent merely upon birth; ...

In Eph 1:5 they are said to have been foreordained unto "adoption as sons" through Jesus Christ, RV; the AV, "adoption of children" is a mistranslation and misleading. God does not "adopt" believers as children; they are begotten as such by His Holy Spirit through faith. "Adoption" is a term involving the dignity of the relationship of believers as sons; it is not a putting into the family by spiritual birth, but a putting into the position of sons. In Rom 8:23 the "adoption" of the believer is set forth as still future, as it there includes the redemption of the body, when the living will be changed and those who have fallen asleep will be raised. In Rom 9:4 "adoption" is spoken of as belonging to Israel, in accordance with the statement in Ex 4:12, "Israel is My Son." Cp. Hosea 11:1. Israel was brought into a special relation with God, a collective relationship, not enjoyed by other nations, Deut 14:1; Jer 31:9, etc.

So, it is important to realize that hoiuthesia is the placing in or the recognition of a son as he has matured. This makes the wording of Ephesians 1:4-5 very significant. "He (God) chose us in Him (Jesus Christ) before the foundation of the world, that we should be holy and without blame before Him (God) in love, having predestined us to adoption (huiothesia) as sons by Jesus Christ to Himself, according to the good pleasure of His will." God has a specific destiny for every believer brought into the family of God by "new birth." That destiny is each one of us growing into Spiritual maturity – being conformed into the very image of Jesus. God does not want us to stop along the way and set up camp. Yes, there is a journey as we grow in Christ but the end of that journey isn't "till we all get to heaven" but rather "till we all come to the unity of the faith and of the knowledge of the Son of God, to a perfect man, to the measure of the stature of the fullness of Christ." (Ephesians 4:13)

The Apostle Peter helps us with this when he writes: "His divine power has granted to us all things that pertain to life and godliness, through the knowledge of Him who called us to His own glory and excellence, by which He has granted to us His precious and very great promises, so that through them you may become <u>partakers</u> of the divine nature...." (2 Peter 1:3-4a NIV)

This word PARTAKERS is the Greek word koinonos. From The Enhanced Strong's Lexicon: 2844 a partner, associate, comrade, companion; sharer, in anything.

So Peter affirms the fact that we are to be partners and sharers in the divine nature.

Isn't it amazing that the Church is waiting for the return of Jesus, but creation is waiting for something completely different? In Romans 8:19-21, the Apostle Paul put it this way. "For the earnest expectation of the creation eagerly waits for the revealing of the sons of God. For the creation was subjected to futility, not willingly, but because of Him who subjected it in hope; because the creation itself also will be delivered from the bondage of corruption into the glorious liberty of the children of God." In verse 19 the ESV says it this way; "For the creation waits with eager longing for the revealing of the sons of God."

So for a quick recap, we all start out as children of God by new birth, then through the help of the Holy Spirit we begin to grow and "...we all, with unveiled face, beholding as in a mirror the glory of the Lord, are being transformed into the same image from glory to glory, just as by the Spirit of the Lord." (2 Corinthians

> *"For the creation waits with eager longing for the revealing of the sons of God."*

3:18) This is the processing of God in our lives as He says in Hebrews 8:10b "I will put My laws in their mind and write them on their hearts; and I will be their God, and they shall be My people." During this time, as friends of God, He is showing us not just His acts but also His ways. Then as we keep pressing into the fullness of Christ we find ourselves being recognized as mature sons in our relationship to our Father God.

Note: Just as the Bride of Christ is made up of both male and female; Sons of God are made up of both male and female.

DISCUSSION QUESTIONS FOR CHAPTER 11

How can you balance being a child (born again) of God and still maintaining the attitude of a servant?

How does your relationship with other Christians and your relationship with God change as you mature?
Babies –

Servant/slave –

Friend –

Son/heir –

How do you see God in each stage and how does God meet you where you are in each stage?
Babies –

Servant/slave –

Friend –

Son/heir –

EQUIPPED

JESUS' EXAMPLE

JUST LIKE JESUS

What does a mature son of God look like? Just like Jesus! From the beginning God's intention has always been to make us like Himself.

Genesis 1:26–27, "Then God said, 'Let Us make man in Our image, according to Our likeness; let them have dominion over the fish of the sea, over the birds of the air, and over the cattle, over all the earth and over every creeping thing that creeps on the earth.' So God created man in His own image; in the image of God He created him; male and female He created them." Here God's purpose for making man is laid out. God created man to be like Himself. I have tried to research the two different words used here, image and likeness, and the best I can come up with is they are synonyms with image emphasizing the physical, i.e. same word image used to refer to an idol and likeness emphasizing the internal, i.e. nature and character.

> *From the beginning God's intention has always been to make us like Himself.*

The idea of becoming just like Jesus is not to take away Jesus' unique position as the only begotten of the Father, the second person of the Trinity, the Lamb of God who takes away the sin of the world; we could go on and on expressing Jesus' differences from us, His brothers. Rather, being transformed into the likeness of Jesus is tied to the concept in Romans 8:29b where the Apostle Paul declares, "That He (Jesus) might be the firstborn among many brethren." Both the uniqueness of Jesus and the reality of His brothers are expressed in Hebrews 2:9–13. "But we see Jesus, who was made a little lower than the angels, for the suffering of death crowned with glory and honor, that He, by the grace of God, might taste death for everyone. For it was fitting for Him (God), for whom are all things and by whom are all things, in bringing many sons to glory, to make the captain of their salvation perfect through sufferings. For both He who sanctifies and those who are being sanctified are all of one, for which reason He is not ashamed to call <u>them brethren</u>, saying: 'I will declare Your name to <u>My brethren</u>; In the midst of the assembly I will sing praise to You.'"

Just recently I was preaching from the book of Hebrews and my research really opened up this thought from a little different perspective. The first chapter in Hebrews focuses on the superiority of Jesus over everything, especially angels. The title of my message was *"Relationship is Better than Ministry or Position."* In verse 4 we read, (Jesus) "having become so much better than the angels, as He has by inheritance obtained a more excellent name than they." As I was reading that verse the phrase "by inheritance" jumped out at me. We all know that Jesus is the Son of God. In fact, John 1:18 declares that Jesus is the "only begotten Son."

> ***Jesus is "one-of-a-kind" and He is the "express image" of His Father.***

ONLY BEGOTTEN – Strong's: 3439 [monogenes]; single of its kind, only; used of only sons or daughters (viewed in relation to their parents).

This word is a compound word made up of Strong's: 3441 [monos]; alone (without a companion), only. We use this word in the English language to mean one. Monorail, monogamy and monolog are among the common English words that begin with mono and mean one. The other part of this compound word is Strong's 1096 [ginomai]; to become, i.e. to come into existence, begin to be, receive being.

This Greek word emphasizes the uniqueness of Jesus. The Message Bible translates John 1:18 this way, "No one has ever seen God, not so much as a glimpse. This one-of-a-kind God-Expression, who exists at the very heart of the Father, has made him plain as day." Jesus is "one-of-a-kind" and He is the "express image" of His Father. (Hebrews 1:3)

Now, consider the word monogenes for a bit. I see two words we use in English. The first word is mono or one-and-only, the second is genes. Webster's College Dictionary gives us this definition for genes: *The basic physical unit of heredity... leads to the expression of hereditary character.*

Here the Scriptures make it very apparent that Jesus Christ is the only one who will ever have the distinctive genes of His Father. Jesus is the one-and-only unique image of His Father. No one else will ever be God's "only begotten Son."

However, as I continued in Hebrews 1:5-6 I read, "For to which of the angels did He ever say: 'You are My Son, Today I have begotten You'? And again: 'I will be to Him a Father, And He shall be to Me a Son'? But when He again brings the firstborn into the world, He says: 'Let all the angels of God worship Him.'" Not only is Jesus the "only begotten Son" of God, He is also the "firstborn." So I looked up the word firstborn.

FIRSTBORN – Strong's: 4416 [prototokos]; the firstborn. This is also a compound word and it combines Strong's word numbers 4413 and 5088.

Strong's: 4413 [protos]; first in time or place; in any succession of things or persons; first in rank; influence or honor.

Strong's: 5088 [tikto]; to bring forth, bear, produce (fruit from the seed); of a woman giving birth; of the earth bringing forth its fruits. metaph. to bear, bring forth.

We use protos in our English word prototype. A prototype is the first with more to follow and a prototype is the pattern for all those that follow. The prototype is unique in that nothing like it has ever existed before it was made but if it is a successful prototype, many more will follow. In the use of this particular Greek word, the writer of Hebrews clearly states that Jesus is unique but that He is also "the firstborn of many brethren" and that His brethren will be made in His image. (Romans 8:29 KJV)

This concept of being made in the image of God/Jesus is reiterated in Romans in a very dramatic way. The Apostle Paul speaks of predestination, a word that means to determine beforehand, in connection with being made in the image of God in Romans 8:29. "For whom He foreknew, He also predestined to be conformed to the image of His Son, that He might be the firstborn among many brethren." Accordingly, we are not truly Jesus' brethren unless we are born again and conformed to His image.

I think we need to talk about predestination here for a little bit. There has been a great divide in the Church through the centuries over predestination vs. free-will. The Bible uses both words and I don't think it is either/or but both. Consider this illustration; suppose my father wants me to move from my home in Missouri to Paradise, California. I have a destiny, predetermined by my father, to end up in Paradise, California. I have never been to Paradise but I have heard wonderful things about it and even have some family and friends who live there. That's predestination. When I leave home, if everything goes OK, I will eventually end up in Paradise. However, along the way, what if I see a sign that advertises an interesting side trip? I can decide to continue on the straight and narrow way to Paradise or I can go on the side trip and check out this fascinating sight. What if I like the sights and living conditions on the side trip more than I think I would like the living conditions in Paradise? I can decide to stop before I get to the destiny my father wants for me. That is freewill. God gave Adam and Eve a choice in the garden as to whom they would obey. God has an awesome destiny determined for each of us, however, we can choose to press on to that destiny or allow ourselves to get sidetracked.

Now, getting back to our main thought. If we were made in the image and likeness of God in the beginning, why does Paul say in Romans 8 that we are chosen by God to be made into Jesus' image? I believe it is because Adam and Eve lost their likeness to God after they disobeyed and God is still working toward His original desire: "Let Us make man in Our image, according to Our likeness..." (Genesis 1:26a) Paul continues this theme in Ephesians 4:13:

> *Our responsibility is to choose to be conformed to His image.*

"...till we all come to the unity of the faith and of the knowledge of the Son of God, to a perfect man, to the measure of the stature of the fullness of Christ."

While I was writing this book, I read a short thought by Bishop Bill Hamon in which he said: "In 2019, the Holy Spirit is beginning an intensified work to purify and perfect us to Christ's likeness and maturity. The final and most important thing to know is this: God's highest calling and purpose for every saint and minister is for them to be conformed to the likeness of Jesus Christ. This is why it is intense. Our responsibility is to choose to be conformed."

God has shown us in His Word that it is His desire for us to be conformed to the image of Jesus Christ. God has given us the Holy Spirit to indwell our lives and help us in this transition. It is time we embrace this very important work of the Holy Spirit.

Explain, in your own words, what Jesus being the "only begotten" and also the "firstborn" means to you.

How is that understanding going to affect your Christian walk?

Since we know that we are predestined to become like Jesus in nature and character; list some areas in your life that are in need of the Holy Spirit's work and then pray for Him to change you.

EQUIPPED

ANOINTED LEADERS

THE WORK OF APOSTLES IN THE CHURCH TODAY

In Ephesians 4:11–13, we get some very specific information from the Apostle Paul about five of the ministries in the Church. Paul also includes a job description for these ministries. "And He Himself gave some to be apostles, some prophets, some evangelists, and some pastors and teachers, for the equipping of the saints for the work of ministry, for the edifying of the body of Christ, till we all come to the unity of the faith and of the knowledge of the Son of God, to a perfect man, to the measure of the stature of the fullness of Christ...."

I understand that many in the Body of Christ today believe that the offices and ministries of the Apostles and Prophets have been done away with. However, as I stated earlier, their job hasn't been completed yet. The Church of Jesus Christ has not fulfilled verse 13, "till we all come to the unity of the faith and of the knowledge of the Son of God, to a perfect man, to the measure of the stature of the fullness of Christ." I firmly believe that the offices and ministries of Apostles and Prophets are not only still with us today but are desperately needed to complete the plan that God has for the Church.

Today most of the Church world uses the term Apostle to mean one or both of the following:

Apostles of the Lamb. - The original twelve disciples (minus Judas plus Matthias) who walked with Jesus and went on to begin the New Testament church.

- Someone (like Paul), not one of the original twelve, sent by God to help spread Christianity.

"The word apostle is a transliterated word, one that is taken directly from another language with little change. In this case, apostle is taken from the common Greek word apostolos. This word literally means one sent forth. Apo literally means from, and stolos comes from stello, which means I send. Within the New Testament and in other classical Greek literature, apostolos has the simple meaning of one sent as representative of another, the representative deriving his authority and power from the one sending him." (Roger Sapp)

The word apostolos is historically a secular term used by the Greeks and the Romans to describe special envoys sent out to establish the dominion of the empire. These envoys were sent to newly acquired territories and charged to subdue, conquer, convert, instruct, train and establish the new subjects in the culture of the empire. Apostles were "sent with the full power and authority of the empire". (John Eckhardt)

God's original mandate to mankind is found in Genesis 1:28. "Then God blessed them, and God said to them, 'Be fruitful and multiply; fill the earth and subdue it; have dominion over the fish of the sea, over the birds of the air, and over every living thing that moves on the earth.'" God told Adam and Eve to "fill the earth and subdue it"; their job would not be finished until the Earth had been filled and subdued. This parallels the command Jesus gave the Church in Matthew 28:18–20. "And Jesus came and spoke to them, saying, 'All authority has been given to Me in heaven and on earth. Go therefore and make

> *God has not changed His plan; He is working through redeemed mankind to finish what He started with Adam and Eve.*

disciples of all the nations, baptizing them in the name of the Father and of the Son and of the Holy Spirit, teaching them to observe all things that I have commanded you; and lo, I am with you always, even to the end of the age.' Amen." God has not changed His plan; He is working through redeemed mankind to finish what He started with Adam and Eve. God reminds us of His desire to have His glory covering the whole Earth again in Numbers 14:20-21. "Then the LORD said: 'I have pardoned, according to your word; but truly, as I live, all the earth shall be filled with the glory of the LORD.'"

Evidence of this earth filled with the glory of the Lord is revealed in Revelation 11:15. "Then the seventh angel sounded: And there were loud voices in heaven, saying, 'The kingdoms of this world have become the kingdoms of our Lord and of His Christ, and He shall reign forever and ever!'" And the work of the Apostles is a major part of how God is bringing this about.

Jesus put Apostles in this world to help new believers become more like Christ as well as to influence the society in which they live.

Jesus said, "You are the salt of the earth. But if the salt loses its saltiness, how can it be made salty again? It is no longer good for anything, except to be thrown out and trampled by men. You are the light of the world. A city on a hill cannot be hidden. Neither do people light a lamp and put it under a bowl. Instead they put it on its stand, and it gives light to everyone in the house." (Matthew 5:13-15 NIV) The much used phrase "we are in the world but not of it" is not a Bible verse but it has influenced us more than many Bible verses have. We have taken it to mean that we should be separate from the world and I would agree with that opinion but we are not to be so separate from the world that we do not influence it. We are supposed to influence this world. We aren't supposed to make the world more Christian by writing more laws. It is essential that we influence the world by changing its culture, winning the lost, and being salt and light in the midst of a "faithless and perverse generation." (Matthew 17:17)

> *Jesus used the same word for how He was sent and how we are sent.*

Not all of us are gifted Apostles but all of us must be involved in changing this world. In John 17:18 (KJV) Jesus said, "As thou (God) hast sent (APOSTELLO) me into the world, even so have I also sent (APOSTELLO) them into the world." Jesus used the same word for how He was sent and how we are sent. Jesus was sent by God with all the authority and power He needed to fulfill His purpose. We have been sent by Jesus with all the authority and power we need to fulfill our purpose. Why haven't we done it yet? Could it be that satan has lied to the Church that the goal of God is just for us to make it to heaven and we have bought into that lie? Could it be that there is a timing of God in this? There are many things we could speculate about but the bottom line is that our job has not been completed so we need to be about our Father's business of expanding the Kingdom of God into all the earth.

In John 20:21 (KJV), Jesus almost repeats Himself: "Then said Jesus to them again, Peace be unto you: as my Father hath sent (APOSTELLO) me, even so send (PEMPO – to insert something of one kind into something of another kind) I you." Here Jesus used a different word for sending us. The point to be made here is that we are not like the world (at least we are not supposed to be) and we are being inserted into it to bring about a change. Jesus' parable about the yeast says it best.

> *Jesus put Apostles in this world to help new believers to become more like Christ as well as to influence the society in which they live.*

"And again He said, 'To what shall I liken the kingdom of God? It is like leaven (yeast), which a woman took and hid in three measures of meal till it was all leavened.'" (Luke 13:20-21) Yeast keeps working until it affects the whole lump. The Church must keep working until the whole world is full of the glory of God.

ADDITIONAL THOUGHTS

Jesus gave Apostles (along with the other gifts/ministries) to the Church to equip the Church to do the work of God on this earth. The job is not finished yet. It is my belief that without true Apostolic influence (not necessarily a resident Apostle) in each Local Church, we cannot fulfill all that God wants us to do in this earth. God gave us ALL of the different gifts so that we will be equipped to do ALL of the work He wants us to do in ALL of the earth.

- Apostles commission and empower the Church to be society changers rather than sheep folds.
- Apostles bring into the Church an undefinable (at least by me) unction that releases a higher level of the presence of God, hence a higher level of His provision.
- Apostles give guidance to the Church as well as to individuals in the Church.
- Apostles and prophets enhance each other's ministries (foundation as well as proclamation).
- Apostles can deal with areas of sin if they aren't being addressed properly by the elders of a Local Church.
- Apostles, as foundational ministries, help in establishing proper doctrine and government in the Church.
- Apostles have a perspective of the big picture in the work of God and may not see and should not be influenced by the politics of a Local Church.
- A final thought, the Church does not understand all that Apostles do, since the Church is lacking in that area.

PROPHETS AND PROPHECY IN THE CHURCH TODAY

Another gift the church misunderstands and doesn't see the current need for today is prophecy. "Why do we need prophets today?" First, I will take you to Ephesians 4:4-16 where they were given by Jesus and again I point out that their job (of bringing the body of Christ to the measure of the stature of the fullness of Christ) is not yet finished. Second, the Prophet Amos declares, "Surely the Lord GOD does nothing, Unless He reveals His secret to His servants the prophets." (Amos 3:7) We believe God is still working in this world, so according to this Scripture God is still working with prophets. Third, from Isaiah 55:11b "(My word) shall not return to Me void, But it shall accomplish what I please, And it shall prosper in the thing for which I sent it" we learn that when prophets are functioning under the true anointing from God and they are speaking God's word to a person or a situation, His power accompanies that word to see it fulfilled. I want to give you some examples from true prophetic ministries that have happened in my life and that can be verified by those who were there when it happened.

A husband and wife team pastored the small Church my family attended when I was in high school. One time in the service the pastoring wife prophesied to me that I was going to preach to thousands of dark skinned people but that these people were not African. I listened to her and didn't know what to think. God had always been an important part of my life but I was going to go to college to become a high school math teacher. In fact, that is exactly what I did and I taught high school math for 2 years before I went into ministry. As time went by, I forgot about that prophesy and eventually became a pastor of a small Church. Many years passed by and then I went to India to minister at a yearly conference of an Indian Apostle who visited our Church about once each year. I had a wonderful time at that conference, where there were over 3000 believers from all over northern India who attended. A few months after I got back home my mother and I were talking about my trip. She reminded me of the prophetic word that had been spoken to me many years before. It was fulfilled exactly as prophesied. Then, ten years later the door opened for my wife and me to minister in Singapore and Indonesia and since then we have preached to thousands more dark-skinned people who are not from Africa. So, you ask, "What's the big deal?" The big deal is that when God spoke through a prophetess He didn't just tell (exhort) me what was going to happen, He released the power to bring His word to pass. Through no effort of mine it did come to pass. In fact, I had been asked to come to India many times and resisted every time without even a thought of that prophesy. Then one time the apostle asked and I felt a nudge in my spirit to say, "Yes". The big deal is that God's personal relationship and care for me was affirmed. The big deal is that the reality of prophesy today was confirmed. The big deal is that I was edified by God's word being confirmed all those years later. The big deal is that I was comforted in knowing that I was in the will of God for my life. And on and on....

Later on in my life I was attending a small fellowship and division had started between some of the members. It was over a particular doctrine and those that accepted it accused those who didn't accept it of being in the flesh, deceived and other not so nice things. On the next Wednesday night I was going to tell the fellowship that my family and I, in good conscience, could not agree with this new doctrine and that we would be leaving so that we would not be a hindrance to what they believed God was speaking into their lives. That afternoon I got a call from my mother that a prophet we knew who had never been to our state had called her and was in the area. He asked if we were having service that night and we were. My mother said, "Don't say anything to Bro. C. L. Moore or to the Church families. Let's wait and see what God does." At the service that night, Bro. Moore preached and prophesied in a kind of overlapping way. One of the things he said was, "This division is not of God." Another word was, "You have received a true word from the Lord but because you have misunderstood it, you are hurting the Body of Christ." I was stunned. Before the service was dismissed, I shared what I was going to do that night. Obviously, I didn't leave. Not after a word like that. We never reconciled the difference of understanding, but a year later, when my wife and I moved, we left with the prayers and blessings of everyone in the fellowship.

I would like to share one more prophecy (of many I could share) concerning a word of the Lord that came to me on my fourth trip to Indonesia. I was at a pastor's conference and the purpose was to encourage and build up village pastors in their relationships to one another and to the Lord. I was at breakfast on the second morning and a sorrowful weight came over me. I heard in my heart that persecution was coming to the Churches in Indonesia. That didn't fit the purpose of the conference and I am not a prophet. I operate in the gift of prophesy sometimes, but this was above my pay grade. I told the Lord, "I can't do this. The gift of prophecy is for edification, exhortation and comfort and this doesn't fit that. This is for someone operating in the office of a prophet." But I couldn't get past the feeling for the next two days. I finally decided to share the warning during my last preaching session. As I shared with the pastors, we prayed that God would intervene and prevent it or minimize the destruction and loss of life. Less than a week later three bombs went off in three different Churches in Surabaya. There were some casualties but not nearly as many as there could have been. More terrorists were killed in the bombings than Christians. This was a true prophetic word from the Lord and I believe that our prayers made a difference.

These experiences and more are why I personally believe that prophecy is for today. Now we will look at the Scriptural reasons to believe that prophecy if for today.

****

The following is an adaptation from teachings and outlines that Roy Ralph has ministered in our home Church and around the world and is used by permission and all Bible references in this section are from the King James Version.

Understanding the relevance of prophecy to the church in the 21st century is imperative. Many would acknowledge the existence of prophets in the Old Testament and possibly even some in the New Testament Church. Yet, are there prophets still today? To answer this question let us look at the Bible and some of the Scriptures that address prophets and prophecy in the early Church. 1 Corinthians 12:28, says "And God hath set some in the church, first apostles, secondarily prophets ..." Also look at Ephesians 4:11 which says, "And he gave some, apostles; and some, prophets; and some, evangelists; and some, pastors and teachers." In 1 Corinthians 14:5 Paul says that he wished that we would all speak with tongues but rather that we would prophesy. It is evident that God placed prophets in the early church. Since God set them in the church, did He take them out? If so, when?

There is no place in the Bible that specifically states that God took Prophets and/or prophecy out of His Church. Many preachers will use 1 Corinthians 13:9-10 as their basis for saying prophets are no longer a part of the church. 1 Corinthians 13:9-10 states, "For we know in part, and we prophesy in part. But when that which is perfect is come, then that which is in part shall be done away."

164

Let us address the two most common arguments that come from this Scripture; they center on what is the perfect and what is the in part that shall be done away.

One consideration for the perfect is the Bible. At the time Paul wrote this letter, the Old Testament part of our Bible was finished and available. If the Bible is the perfect thing, then why didn't Paul write, "When Scripture is completed," or even "When that which is perfect is completed"?

If the perfect is the Bible, then which translation is it? There are many translations in many different languages and that is what they are – translations. Unless you are reading copies of the original Greek and Hebrew you simply have a translation and translations are not perfect; translations represent the translator's understanding of the original writings. I believe that having a translation of the Bible in your native language is important for studying. Additional translations can help create a clear comprehension by comparing passages between translations to help you understand the full meaning of the original. So, if the Bible is the perfect that we are looking for, we have to rely only upon the original Hebrew and Greek manuscripts.

Some say what is perfect is Jesus and that is true, Jesus is perfect, but is He the perfect thing that Paul is talking about? At the time of this writing, Jesus had ascended to the right hand of the Father many years before. Paul talks about prophets in the Church he was a part of (Acts 13:1), so if that which is perfect refers to Jesus, it must be His second coming - which we are still looking forward to.

In 1 Corinthians 13 in addition to prophesying in part, it also says that we know in part. So if the in part passes away when the perfect comes then we will know everything fully. I am not aware that there is anyone who suggests that knowledge has passed away or that we now have all knowledge. So if knowledge is still with us even though just in part, prophecy is still with us even though just in part.

The only other Scripture that I know of that people use to argue that prophets and prophecy have ceased is Revelation 22:18-19. There it says that if someone adds to the Book of Revelation, God will add to him the plagues written in the Book of Revelation. Also if anyone takes away from the words of the Book God would take away his part out of the Book of Life. No true Prophet believes that his prophecy needs to be added to the Book of Revelation, rather that current prophecy stands apart from the Bible and is to be judged by the Bible.

This brings me to the conclusion that God has not removed prophets and prophecy from the Church; therefore both are still valid for today.

It is important to understand that there are different levels of prophecy in the New Testament Church.
It needs to be pointed out that not all who prophesy are Prophets. In the New Testament, prophecy operates on three levels.

The Spirit of prophecy (God can release prophecy through any believer)
It is in Revelation 19:10 that we see these exact words. "And I fell at his feet to worship him. But he said to me, 'See that you do not do that! I am your fellow servant, and of your brethren who have the testimony of Jesus. Worship God! For the testimony of Jesus is the spirit of prophecy.'"

> *Everyone can be used through the Spirit of prophecy but not everyone who prophesies will have the gift of prophecy.*

The Spirit of prophecy is speaking of the Holy Spirit's mantle of anointing given to every born-again believer, which enables him to prophesy like Saul in 1 Samuel 10:6, 9-11. "Then the Spirit of the LORD will come upon you, and you will prophesy with them and be turned into another man. ...So it was, when he had turned his back to go from Samuel, that God gave him another heart; and all those signs came to pass that day. When they came there to the hill, there was a group of prophets to meet him; then the Spirit of God came upon him, and he prophesied among them. And it happened, when all who knew him formerly saw that he indeed prophesied among the prophets, that the people said to one another, 'What is this that has come upon the son of Kish? Is Saul also among the prophets?'" Saul did not become a Prophet at this time, it was only because the Holy Spirit came upon him that he could prophecy. This is evidenced again in 1 Samuel 19:18-24.

In the New Testament the Apostle Paul tells us in 1 Corinthians 14:31 "… you can all prophesy one by one, that all may learn and all may be encouraged." All may prophesy but some can only prophesy when the mantle comes upon them and they respond in faith to the still small voice of the Lord in their hearts.

This type of prophecy operates around true Prophets or when a Spirit of prophecy is moving in a church service in an atmosphere of worship and praise with strong leadership present.

The Gift of prophecy (One of the Gifts of the Spirit)
Alongside the Spirit of prophecy is the gift of prophecy. It is a higher realm of prophecy and conveys a greater responsibility for the one prophesying. (Romans 12:6 and 1 Corinthians 12:4) This gift is one of the gifts of the Spirit that the Apostle Paul wrote about in 1 Corinthians 12:7–11. "But the manifestation of the Spirit is given to each one for the profit of all: for to one is given the word of wisdom through the Spirit, to another the word of knowledge through the same Spirit, to another faith by the same Spirit, to another gifts of healings by the same Spirit, to another the working of miracles, to another prophecy, to another discerning of spirits, to another different kinds of tongues, to another the interpretation of tongues. But one and the same Spirit works all these things, distributing to each one individually as He wills." Here we see that the Holy Spirit gives the gift of prophecy to those He chooses. Everyone can be used through the Spirit of prophecy but not everyone who prophesies will have the gift of prophecy. The Holy Spirit gives this gift to those He chooses. The person with the gift of prophecy can prophesy on a somewhat regular basis.

The Office of Prophet – (Five Fold Ministry Prophet)
Ephesians 4:11 And He Himself (Jesus Christ) gave some, apostles; some, prophets; some, evangelists; and some, pastors and teachers.

The Lord ordains these types of prophets, not man - though man may lay hands on them; and recognize their calling, the calling itself comes from God alone.

Some examples of this from the Old Testament:

Jeremiah 1:5 "Before I formed you in the womb I knew you..."

Amos 7:15 Then the LORD took me as I followed the flock, And the LORD said to me, '"Go, prophesy to My people Israel."

Some examples in the New Testament:

Acts 13:1 Now in the church that was at Antioch there were certain prophets and teachers....

Acts 11:27–28 And in these days prophets came from Jerusalem to Antioch....

Acts 21:10–11 And as we stayed many days, a certain prophet named Agabus came down from Judea....

God can use those who function in the Office of a Prophet to root out; pull down; destroy; throw down; build; plant as per Jeremiah 1:10. A Prophet can also move in revelatory, predictive, corrective, direction, and etc. These prophecies should be judged by other Prophets and confirmed in the mouth of two or three witnesses as well as in the heart of the one prophesied to. We know in part and we prophesy in part; that is why prophecy is to be judged.

All true prophecy is from God, but God himself ordains those who walk in the Office of a Prophet.

****

The Function of Prophecy

All who prophesy will fulfill one or more of these three functions from 1 Corinthians 14:3, "But he who prophesies speaks edification and exhortation and comfort to men."

Edification – Prophecy is used to build up and strengthen an individual or a Church in their Spiritual growth and relationship with God. No true prophetic ministry will cut down or tear down God's people or Church; even a rebuke will be done in a manner that brings restoration. See Jeremiah 1

Exhortation – Prophecy is used to give instruction as well as admonition and warning to individuals, Churches, and nations.

Comfort – Prophecy is used to bring comfort or consolation to individuals, Churches and nations in times of trials, afflictions, etc.

These three functions will operate in all three realms of prophecy (Spirit of prophecy, Gift of prophecy, and the Office of a Prophet).

This brings us to an important distinction between Old Testament Prophets and New Testament Prophets. In the Old Testament, the Prophet was judged as a true or false Prophet, in the New Testament, prophecy brought by true followers of Jesus is judged as a true or false prophecy. 1 Corinthians 14:29 says, "Let two or three prophets speak, and let the others judge." Jesus warns of false prophets, but those who are truly false prophets are not followers of Jesus.

Just recently a group of Pastors visit us from France. They ministered some prophetic words to members of our Church. As they did, they used the following pattern as a sample of how to follow up a personal prophecy. I believe it is an excellent tool to help prophecy be accepted, not just heard.

FIVE QUESTIONS after you receive a prophetic word:

1. What did you hear?
   About half of those receiving prophetic words don't remember everything the person said.
2. What did you understand?
   Were the words or images clear to you? It isn't necessarily bad if everything isn't understood. Sometimes more understanding comes later.
3. Is there a timeline indicated in the prophetic word?
   Immediate is not the same as: I, the Lord, will do...
4. Who does what? What is uniquely God's responsibility and what is uniquely your responsibility? Example: God's part, God calls you to the mission field; your part, learn the language, make the necessary preparations, pack your bags.
5. How do you feel about the prophetic word?
   Did it witness in your heart? If not, put it on the shelf and wait for conformation.

I will not take the time to write about the functions of Evangelists, Pastors, and Teachers in the Church because most of us see them in action on a daily or weekly basis.

(If you are interested in knowing more about prophetic ministry, I suggest you get the book, "All May Prophesy – Understanding Prophecy" by Roy Ralph. It is available on Amazon.com)

DISCUSSION QUESTIONS FOR CHAPTER 13

Even though you might not be an apostle you are to be salt and light in the world. How does that change your approach to Christian living?

Have you seen a Prophet at work? How did their word fulfill one of these three functions?

PART IV

THE MISSION CHANGING THE WORLD

CHANGING THE WORLD

All this equipping was to enable Jesus' disciples to carry out the mission of birthing, building, and establishing Jesus' Church. Jesus said that He would build His Church, however it wasn't to be built by His direct earthly supervision but by His gifted ministry with the divine help of the Holy Spirit. Today the development of this Church of Jesus Christ is still a work in progress. God is still equipping His people for the work of the ministry. "And He (Jesus) Himself gave some to be apostles, some prophets, some evangelists, and some pastors and teachers, for the equipping of the saints for the work of ministry...." (Ephesians 4:11–12)

The Church has a mission that begins at Salvation, continues with equipping the Saints and isn't finished until the whole world is touched with the Gospel. Matthew 28:18–20 says, "And Jesus came and spoke to them, saying, 'All authority has been given to Me in heaven and on earth. Go therefore and make disciples of all the nations, baptizing them in the name of the Father and of the Son and of the Holy Spirit, teaching them to observe all things that I have commanded you; and lo, I am with you always, even to the end of the age.' Amen."

Mark 16:15, 17–18 expands upon that mission a little, "And He said to them, 'Go into all the world and preach the gospel to every creature.... And these signs will follow those who believe: In My name they will cast out demons; they will speak with new tongues; they will take up serpents; and if they drink anything deadly, it will by no means hurt them; they will lay hands on the sick, and they will recover.'"

Luke, in Acts 1:6–8, emphasizes the universality of this mission: "But you shall receive power when the Holy Spirit has come upon you; and you shall be witnesses to Me in Jerusalem, and in all Judea and Samaria, and to the end of the earth."

And Matthew declares that God's purpose for His Church on this Earth will not be complete until the entire world is reached. Matthew 24:14 "And this gospel of the kingdom will be preached in all the world as a witness to all the nations, and then the end will come."

Notice that in this Scripture Jesus says, "the gospel of the kingdom". Jesus is not talking only about the good news of Salvation. He is talking about the good news of the fullness of God's kingdom as it touches every aspect of our lives and every part of this Earth. God is calling us to put our shoulder to the plow, to take this good news, and not look back until His work is finished! (Luke 9:62)

BEING ABOUT THE
FATHER'S BUSINESS

Luke 19:11–14 (KJV) "And as they heard these things, he (Jesus) added and spake a parable, because he was nigh to Jerusalem, and because they thought that the kingdom of God should immediately appear. He said therefore, 'A certain nobleman went into a far country to receive for himself a kingdom, and to return. And he called his ten servants, and delivered them ten pounds, and said unto them, "Occupy till I come." But his citizens hated him, and sent a message after him, saying, "We will not have this man to reign over us."'"

What did Jesus mean when He said, "Occupy"? The word here does not mean mark time, fill a seat, or relax until I come. This word occupy is Strong's: 4231 [pragmateuomai]; to be occupied in anything; to carry on a business. The only translation that I have access to that uses the word occupy here is the King James Version; all the other versions I have use some form of a word that emphasizes the idea of being busy. The Message Bible says, "Operate with this until I return," the New Living Translation says: "Invest this for me while I am gone," the New King James Version says, "Do business till I come," the English Standard Version says, "Engage in business until I come," and Young's

> *Jesus said that we were to be about His business until He returns.*

Literal Translation says, "Do business—till I come...." All of these translations point out occupy as an action verb.

The next question, a very important one, is "What business are we to be about?" Jesus answered that for us when He was 12 years old. In Luke 2:48–49 we read, "So when they saw Him, they were amazed; and His mother said to Him, 'Son, why have You done this to us? Look, Your father and I have sought You anxiously.' And He said to them, 'Why did you seek Me? Did you not know that I must be about My Father's business?'" And since Jesus told us in Matthew 23:9, "Do not call anyone on earth your father; for One is your Father, He who is in heaven." We know that being about our Father's business is being about God's business. All of the facets of these two questions are more than we can consider here but we can at least look at some of the aspects of being occupied with our Father's business.

Jesus declares in John 5:36 (NLT) that the works His Father gave Him to do were teaching and miracles. "But I have a greater witness than John—my teachings and my miracles. The Father gave me these works to accomplish, and they prove that he sent me." The American Church is great at the work of teaching but we have fallen behind in the working of miracles. Both of these, and more, are works that the Father has given us to do as we eagerly await Jesus' return.

> **God has never stopped being a supernatural God, we just stopped expecting it.**

A number of years ago I shared from the pulpit that God didn't need to do anything more for me to prove His love for me. He showed the greatness of His love in giving His life for me on the cross and He has blessed me and my family very much over the years. That sounds kind of spiritual but God showed me it was wrong thinking. One day as I was praying in the back of our sanctuary, I found myself quoting Paul's words in 1 Corinthians 2:4, "And my speech and my preaching were not with persuasive words of human wisdom, but in demonstration of the Spirit and of power...." It shocked me. I had been walking back and forth and I stopped in my tracks and thought, "where did that come from?" I had made the decision that teaching and growing in the grace and knowledge of God was God's purpose for us at this time, not demonstrations of His power. As I questioned God, I heard Him say these words, "I have never stopped being a supernatural God, you just stopped expecting it." What a rebuke! But what a wonderful Father who would not let me continue in a false understanding of how He wants to work in this world.

Not only did Jesus go about healing the sick, raising the dead, casting out demons and more; He sent us to do the same thing in Mark 16:15–18, "And He said to them, 'Go into all the world and preach the gospel to every creature. He who believes and is baptized will be saved; but he who does not believe will be condemned. And these signs will follow those who believe: In My name they will cast out demons; they will speak with new tongues; they will take up serpents; and if they drink anything deadly, it will by no means hurt them; they will lay hands on the sick, and they will recover.'"

John 14:12–13 "Most assuredly, I say to you, he who believes in Me, the works that I do he will do also; and greater works than these he will do, because I go to My Father. And whatever you ask in My name, that I will do, that the Father may be glorified in the Son."

We know healings and miracles did not end with Jesus or with His disciples. Most Christian denominations have wonderful testimonies of healings and other miracles in their formative years and in the histories of their missionaries as they took the Gospel to the lost, especially in what are now termed Third-World countries. Why don't we expect miracles in the Western world? I'm not sure about anyone else but I stopped expecting them because they were not happening. I was wrong. Now, I can boast in the Lord and tell you that I have seen more miracles in the last 10 years of my life than I had seen in my whole life up to that time. It would be good to point out that the first notable thing that happened in the book of Acts after the Baptism of the Holy Spirit was the salvation of 3000 Jews. The second notable thing that happened was the lame man at the Temple walking and leaping and praising God! The third notable thing that happened was the Church in Acts 4:29–30 prayed, "Now, Lord, look on their threats, and grant to Your servants that with all boldness they may speak Your word, by stretching out Your hand to heal, and that signs and wonders may be done through the name of Your holy Servant Jesus." The first prayer recorded in the book of Acts was a prayer for boldness for the miraculous.

I remember as a child reading the book "Living to tell of Death" written by a teen-aged girl who was raised from the dead in Mississippi in the late 1940's. Her married name was Lura Grubb and she ministered with her husband Paul Grubb for many years in Memphis, Tennessee. All my growing up years, she is the only one that I ever heard of being raised from the dead. Then just a few years ago, just after John Smith (Ruiz) died by drowning in the St. Louis area in 2015 and came back from the dead through the prayers of his mother, I realized in the last few of years I had read about five or six other people being raised from the dead. Are miracles on the increase or are we just hearing about them more?

We are called by God to be about His business as we wait for Jesus' return.

In the extended period of time from Jesus' ascension to His return, specific things are to take place. In His parables, Jesus told us that this time was for Him to receive His kingdom. David, in Psalm 110:1-4, tells us about this time. "The Lord said to my Lord, 'Sit at My right hand, Till I make Your enemies Your footstool.' The Lord shall send the rod of Your strength out of Zion. Rule in the midst of Your enemies! Your people shall be volunteers (willing) In the day of Your power.'" During this time God is putting satan under the feet of Jesus but how is He doing this? Paul, writing to the Church in Rome, says it this way: "And the God of peace will crush satan under your feet shortly...." (Romans 16:20a) God has purposed to use His Church to put satan and all his works under the feet of Jesus. And we must be about our Father's business.

In Jesus' parables, there is a reoccurring thought that Jesus was going to be gone for a long time. This is especially true in Matthew

25 in the parables of the Talents and The Ten Virgins. In the parable of the talents it says, "after a long time the master returned" and in the parable of the ten virgins they waited so long that they all (both wise and foolish) fell asleep. So we have to be careful that we don't get discouraged and become like the servant in Matthew 24:48b, "(the) evil servant says in his heart, 'My master is delaying his coming,'" and begins to mistreat his fellow servants and becomes corrupt in his lifestyle. But we need to remember Galatians 6:9, "And let us not grow weary while doing good, for in due season we shall reap if we do not lose heart." We need to be convinced that even though it appears that nothing's ever going to change; Jesus is coming back and that the promise of Revelation 11:15 (KJV), "And the seventh angel sounded; and there were great voices in heaven, saying, The kingdoms of this world are become the kingdoms of our Lord, and of his Christ; and he shall reign for ever and ever" will be fulfilled!

MORE OF GOD'S BUSINESS

A major part of God's work here on the earth is to destroy the works of the devil. In 1 John 3:8 we read, "He who sins is of the devil, for the devil has sinned from the beginning. For this purpose the Son of God was manifested, that He might destroy the works of the devil." Just about everything Jesus did was connected with destroying the work of the devil. From preaching the Gospel, to healing the sick, to casting out devils, to raising the dead; He was working to destroy the work of satan. Jesus himself said it this way: "for the Son of Man has come to seek and to save that which was lost." (Luke 19:10)

What was lost? A life lived in the presence of God, in fellowship with God, for the purpose of God, by the power of God, free from all of the consequences of a fallen world.

Who lost it? Adam and Eve.
When was it lost? In the beginning.
Where was it lost? In the garden.
Why was it lost? Because of disobedience to God.

> *A major part of God's work here on the earth is to destroy the works of the devil.*

Originally God gave mankind a job. In Genesis 1:26 we read, "Then God said, 'Let Us make man in Our image, according to Our likeness; let them have dominion over the fish of the sea, over the birds of the air, and over the cattle, over all the earth and over every creeping thing that creeps on the earth.'" In my research it appears that the New Living Translation of Genesis 1:26 has an equally valid rendering of the words "let them have dominion". It reads this way: "Then God said, 'Let us make human beings in our image, to be like us. <u>They will reign</u> over the fish in the sea, the birds in the sky, the livestock, all the wild animals on the earth, and the small animals that scurry along the ground.'" So we see here that the NLT expresses emphatically that mankind will have dominion. It is not a case of getting God's permission to have dominion but it is God's declared will for mankind to have dominion over the earth.

Two verses later in Genesis 1:28 I believe God gave Adam and Eve directions on how to fulfill this mission. "Then God blessed them, and God said to them, 'Be fruitful and multiply; fill the earth and subdue it; have dominion over the fish of the sea, over the birds of the air, and over every living thing that moves on the earth.'" I know that one of the Hebrew patterns of writing was to use doublets or two words together that were synonyms. That might be the case here with fruitful and multiply along with fill and subdue but I would like to look at these words as the blueprint of how Adam and Eve were to move into dominion in the whole earth.

> *God's gifts are not trophies to be set on a shelf and admired; they are tools for the advancement of God's kingdom.*

Be fruitful – have children
Strong's: 6509 [parah]; to bear fruit, be fruitful, branch off.

Genesis 17:5b–6 "... for I have made you a father of many nations. I will make you exceedingly fruitful; and I will make nations of you, and kings shall come from you." The word fruitful in Genesis 1:28 is the same word used here in Genesis 17:6

Multiply – to increase with children as well as other ways, plentiful, to increase greatly
Strong's: 7235 [rabah]; 1 be or become great, be or become many, be or become much, be or become numerous; to make large, enlarge, increase, become many; 2 to shoot

So as a doublet this could be a synonym to fruitful, but it is also used in other ways. The same word for multiply is translated as abundant in Psalm 130:7: "O Israel, hope in the LORD; For with the LORD there is mercy, And with Him is <u>abundant</u> redemption."

This word "MULTIPLY" (rabah) in Brown, Driver, Briggs, Hebrew and English Lexicon #8050: shooting, the action of hurling a flying object with a taut instrument (a bow)

The whole purpose of a bow is to multiply the strength and accuracy of the archer.

This word is used again in Genesis 21:20 "So God was with the lad; and he grew and dwelt in the wilderness, and became an archer." Here the better translation would be "and grew in ability as an archer."

Thus the word for multiply in Genesis 1:28 could be applied to multiplying not just children but mankind's knowledge, abilities, strength, etc.

So this word, multiply, holds in it much more than just having lots of children. We are fulfilling this Scripture when we grow in knowledge and abilities both in the Spiritual and the natural. I believe God is especially pleased as we study His Word and search out its depths. We not only need to hide His Word in our hearts so we won't sin against Him (Psalms 119:11), but we also need to engraft His Word into our very lives so that our lives reflect His nature and character. God is also pleased as we grow in our abilities to operate in our gifts and callings. Hebrews 5:14a tells us, "But solid food belongs to those who are of full age, that is, those who by reason of use have their senses exercised...." God wants us to use the gifts He has given us. Remember, God's gifts are not trophies to be set on a shelf and admired nor are they for personal gain; they are tools that God has given us for the advancement of His kingdom.

<table>
<tr><td>

Jesus came to get mankind back in right relationship with God and on the right track in fulfilling God's purposes.

</td><td>

Fill – fill up
Enhanced Strong's Lexicon: 4390 [male']; to fill, be full; fullness, abundance (participle); to be full, be accomplished, be ended; to consecrate, fill the hand.

</td></tr>
</table>

Fill is used again in these verses: Genesis 21:19 (speaking of Hagar), "Then God opened her eyes, and she saw a well of water. And she went and <u>filled</u> the skin with water, and gave the lad a drink." And in Genesis 25:24 (speaking of Rebekah), "So when her days were <u>fulfilled</u> for her to give birth, indeed there were twins in her womb." It basically means to fill something full.

Subdue it – conquer and control. Strong's: 3533 [kabash]; to subject, subdue, force, keep under, bring into bondage; make subservient.

SUBDUE in the Theological Wordbook of the Old Testament #951 means to: overcome, enslave, i.e., conquer and control an environment or people

Here are two more Scriptures that use the word subdue. Joshua 18:1 "Now the whole congregation of the children of Israel assembled together at Shiloh, and set up the tabernacle of meeting there. And the land was <u>subdued</u> before them." And 2 Samuel 8:11 "King David also dedicated these to the LORD, along with the silver and gold that he had dedicated from all the nations which he had <u>subdued</u>—".

The word for subdue holds in itself the idea of struggle. Adam and Eve were given the Garden of Eden but they were to subdue the rest of the world. This idea of subduing the rest of the world is repeated in the conquering of Canaan's land by Israel. God told the Israelites that He would give them the land. Then God told Israel to go and make it happen. "I will send My fear before you, I will cause confusion among all the people to whom you come, and will make all your enemies turn their backs to you. And I will send hornets before you.... Little by little I will drive them out from before you, until you have increased, and you inherit the land." (Exodus 23:27–30)

Mankind was given the task of subduing the earth outside the Garden of Eden. God gave mankind a job. God could have done it all Himself but He created mankind with a desire and need to be useful, to be productive, to overcome difficult situations. Interestingly enough, God didn't only call the Garden of Eden good; when He created the heavens and the earth He saw that all He had created was good. Inside this good earth, God made a garden, a little piece of Heaven on earth, and put mankind in it to experience what the rest of the world should be like. Then God told Adam He had a task for him; one that would take quite a long time to accomplish. God gave Adam a task and a helper, Eve, who was just right to help Adam finish his task. God then gave Adam and Eve the plan:

1. <u>Be fruitful</u>, have lots of children, both physical and spiritual.

2. <u>Multiply</u> in the number of your children but also in knowledge, abilities, strength, etc. Then as you increase in these areas you will be ready to...

3. <u>Fill</u> the rest of the Earth to the full with your children and with the knowledge of God. And be sure to...

4. <u>Subdue</u> the Earth. Fill the Earth with the government of God. Don't just add your descendants and knowledge to what is already there; change what is there. In other words, expand the Garden of Eden until it covers the whole world.

After the fall, God's plan didn't change. It just had to wait for fulfillment until Jesus came and got mankind back in right relationship

> *Creation is not waiting for the coming of the Lord but for the people of God to come to their full maturity in Christ.*

with God and on the right track in fulfilling God's purposes.

Did you ever stop to think about how much the rest of God's creation was impacted by the sin of mankind? Just one small example: what were mosquitos like before the fall — what was their purpose? Consider this: the creation is not waiting for the coming of the Lord but for the people of God to come to their full maturity in Christ Jesus. Romans 8:19–22 (ESV) says it this way, "For the creation waits with eager longing for the revealing of the sons of God. For the creation was subjected to futility, not willingly, but because of him who subjected it, in hope that the creation itself will be set free from its bondage to corruption and obtain the freedom of the glory of the children of God. For we know that the whole creation has been groaning together in the pains of childbirth until now." We have no idea how much corruption the earth is enduring right now because of sin. Creation itself is waiting for God' sons to be revealed so it can be free from the corruption it is under.

> *Pray the Lord's Prayer and then be about the Father's business of subduing satan and releasing God's kingdom into the earth.*

Mankind is right back where we were when God first sent Adam out into the world to subdue it. Jesus put it this way; "In this manner, therefore, pray: Our Father in heaven, Hallowed be Your name. Your kingdom come. Your will be done on earth as it is in heaven." (Matthew 6:9–10) It is still the will and plan of God for His kingdom to fill this earth. John in the book of Revelation tells us of a future time when this declaration will be shouted in the heavens: "The kingdom of the world has become the kingdom of our Lord and of his Christ, and he shall reign forever and ever." (Revelation 11:15 ESV)

Right now we are in the in-between time. We are between praying Jesus' prayer and seeing His prayer fulfilled. The reality is that we are not just supposed to pray the prayer and wait for God to do something. Pray the Lord's Prayer and then be about the Father's business of subduing satan and releasing God's kingdom into the earth.

Remember God's declaration in Isaiah 9:7, "Of the increase of His government and peace There will be no end, Upon the throne of David and over His kingdom, To order it and establish it with judgment and justice From that time forward, even forever. The zeal of the LORD of hosts will perform this." And then in Numbers 14:20-21 (KJV), "And (speaking to Moses) the LORD said, 'I have pardoned according to thy word: But as truly as I live, all the earth shall be filled with the glory of the LORD.'"

By seeking first the kingdom of God with our whole heart and sharing it with those around us; by reaching out to a lost and dying world both at home and abroad with a heart of love; by being salt and light in our neighborhood and cities, we are working with God to see His kingdom come and His will being done on Earth as it is in Heaven

I have started ending the PowerPoint presentations of my sermons by putting this slide on the screen. The whole Church recites this together:

I am a son/daughter of God.

Jesus is my Savior and I have been empowered by the Holy Spirit.

I have been brought into the world for such a time as this.

I came today to grow in my relationship with Jesus and to be refreshed by and refilled with the Holy Spirit.

With God as my strength, I go out into this lost and dying world to be salt and light.

As a bearer of the love of God, I go out into this world to bring hope to the hopeless, strength to the weak, joy to the sorrowful, healing to the hurting and salvation to the lost.

I will work together with God to change this world one person at a time.

DISCUSSION QUESTIONS FOR CHAPTER 14

As a Christian how should you go about your Father's business during your time on earth?

How can you destroy the work of the devil?

Have you seen an increase in the miraculous?

What do you think it would be like to actually abide in the presence of God?

How can you live in the presence of God and carry it with you as you go about your daily life?

How can you bring God's presence and be more aware of God's presence in your church?

SHOWING FORTH HIS GLORY

God is awesome! In fact He is so far beyond awesome that we don't have words to adequately express how awesome He really is. However, God enables us to partner with Him to show some of His awesomeness (glory) with our words and our actions. "But you are a chosen generation, a royal priesthood, a holy nation, His own special people, that you may proclaim the praises of Him who called you out of darkness into His marvelous light." (1 Peter 2:9)

Showing forth the glory of God is also a part of the mission of the Church. We are not only supposed to praise God with our lips but our lives should be lived to give God glory. Jesus said, "Let your light so shine before men, that they may see your good works and glorify your Father in heaven." (Matthew 5:16) Paul added, "that we who first trusted in Christ should be to the praise of His glory." (Ephesians 1:12) I have taught for a long time that Christians are always showing either the grace or the glory of God. We show the grace of God when we are living below God's standards yet still living in God's love, and we are showing the glory of God

> *So if the old way, which has been replaced, was glorious, how much more glorious is the new, which remains forever!*

when we are living in God's presence and endeavoring to live overcoming lives in this world. Make a determination to live for His glory!

As you read the following Scripture, make note of how many times the word glory is used and consider the contrast between the glory of the Old and New Covenant. "The old way, with laws etched in stone, led to death, though it began with such glory that the people of Israel could not bear to look at Moses' face. For his face shone with the glory of God, even though the brightness was already fading away. Shouldn't we expect far greater glory under the new way, now that the Holy Spirit is giving life? If the old way, which brought condemnation, was glorious, how much more glorious is the new way, which makes us right with God! In fact, that first glory was not glorious at all compared with the overwhelming glory of the new way. So if the old way, which has been replaced, was glorious, how much more glorious is the new, which remains forever!" (2 Corinthians 3:7-11 NLT) The testimony that the Church of Jesus Christ is living in the fullness of the blessings of the New Covenant is showing this glory. We are to be a glorious Church glorifying God in all our ways.

The Apostle Paul writes, "To me, who am less than the least of all the saints, this grace was given, that I should preach among the Gentiles the unsearchable riches of Christ, ... to the intent that now the manifold wisdom of God might be made known by the church to the principalities and powers in the heavenly places, according to the eternal purpose which He accomplished in Christ Jesus our Lord." (Ephesians 3:8 & 10-11) It is amazing that God uses His Church to show His wisdom to principalities and powers not just on the earth but also in heavenly places and not just in the future but now! We have no idea what impact our earthly actions have in the heavenly realm, but Jesus told us this in Matthew 18:18, "Assuredly, I say to you, whatever you bind on earth will be bound in heaven, and whatever you loose on earth will be loosed in heaven." That Church, that glorious Church is the woman spoken of in Revelation 12:1, "a great wonder in heaven" and she gives all the glory to God.

Knowing that giving glory to God is an important part of the mission of the Church, what are some of the things that the Bible says bring God glory?

Read the story of Lazarus (John 11) and ask yourself the following questions.

1. Why did Jesus stay away when He found out that Lazarus, a very dear friend, was sick?

2. What did Jesus say the purpose of this sickness was?

The first question is answered in verse 15a. "And I am glad for your sakes that I wasn't there. You're about to be given new grounds for believing." (TMB) And then in the NLT: "And for your sakes, I'm glad I wasn't there, for now you will really believe." Jesus saw this event as a way to really strengthen the faith of His disciples.

I believe Jesus also stayed away because He loved Mary, Martha and Lazarus so much that it would have been very hard for Him to watch them suffer and grieve over Lazarus' sickness and eventual death. Mary and Martha did not understand why Jesus wouldn't heal their brother when He had healed so many others. They would have needlessly suffered the rejection that would have come from Jesus' refusal to help.

In verses 3 and 4 we find the answer to the second question. Jesus explained to His disciples that Lazarus was not going to die from this sickness but that it was for the glory of God and for Jesus' own glory. Well, we know Lazarus did die from this sickness, but his death was not permanent.

Jesus loved and had great compassion for Mary, Martha and Lazarus in Lazarus' sickness but He knew by direct revelation from the Father that the glory God wanted out of this situation was going to be much more than just (if I can even use that word) another healing. Remember that Jesus only did what He saw the Father do; so He must have seen His Father waiting for Lazarus to die. The glory God wanted from this situation was the glory that would come from raising someone who had been dead for four days.

I don't want to be gross here, but can you imagine how far the decay had advanced in Lazarus' body if the stench of it over-powered the spices and ointments that they had put on his body after he died? To put it plainly, Lazarus' body was rotting. The massive amount of reconstruction of Lazarus' flesh, nerves and brain cells is beyond my grasp. The miracle of restoring everything that was destroyed in Lazarus' body as he began to decay is the greater glory God wanted to display and display it He did!

In the story of the paralytic let down through the roof we see that the religious leaders of Jesus' day were very upset that Jesus told the paralytic that his sins were forgiven but it was when Jesus healed this paralyzed man that the multitudes, "… marveled and glorified God, who had given such power to men." (Matthew 9:6-8)

"And great multitudes came unto him, having with them those that were lame, blind, dumb, maimed, and many others, and cast them down at Jesus' feet; and he healed them: Insomuch that the multitude wondered, when they saw the dumb to speak, the maimed to be whole, the lame to walk, and the blind to see: and they glorified the God of Israel." (Matthew 15:30-31 KJV)

In Luke 13:11-13 we read, "And behold, there was a woman who had a spirit of infirmity eighteen years, and was bent over and could in no way raise herself up. But when Jesus saw her, He called her to Him and said to her, 'Woman, you are loosed from your infirmity.' And He laid His hands on her, and immediately she was made straight, and glorified God." This woman didn't glorify God that she had been able to endure with patience and grace eighteen years of suffering. She glorified God when she was healed! Jesus made it very plain in verse 16 where this infirmity came from when He said, "So ought not this woman, being a daughter of Abraham, whom satan has bound—think of it—for eighteen years, be loosed from this bond on the Sabbath?"

If a situation has satan's fingerprints all over it, don't blame it on God. Satan came to "steal, kill and destroy" (John 10:10) but Jesus came to destroy the works of the devil (1 John 3:8) and bring abundant life to those who believe. So, when we are doing the Father's business of destroying any and all of the works of the devil, we are giving Glory to our awesome God! And we are opening the way to have all creation join us as we give Him praise for His wondrous works!

QUESTIONS FOR CHAPTER 15

Like in the story of Lazarus, can you look back in your life and see how God delayed His answer to a need you had prayed about and it brought greater glory to Him?

If so, describe the situation.

Can you think of other examples in the New Testament where miracles happened and the glory was given directly to Jesus or God?

BECOMING A GLORIOUS CHURCH

A BRIDE FIT FOR THE SON OF GOD

In the Old Testament, God spoke of Israel as His bride and God as the husband. In Isaiah 54:5a God declares, "For your Maker is your husband, The LORD of hosts is His name..." Also, in Jeremiah 3:14 we read, "'Return, O backsliding children,' says the LORD; 'for I am married to you.'" God's heart has always been to draw us to an intimate relationship of fellowship with him. The Song of Solomon is full of this imagery. "Draw me, we will run after thee: The king hath brought me into his chambers...." (Song of Solomon 1:4a)

In Ezekiel 16:9-14 God talks about how He took Israel from her nakedness and turned her into a beautiful bride. But as good as God was to them, the Israelites chose to worship other gods. As you read on in Ezekiel 16:31-32, God told Israel, "You erected your shrine at the head of every road, and built your high place in every street. Yet you were not like a harlot, because you scorned payment. You are an adulterous wife, who takes strangers instead of her husband." This is confirmed in Jeremiah 31:32, "not according to the covenant that I made with their fathers in the day that I took them by the hand to lead them out of the land of Egypt, My covenant which they broke, though I was a husband to them, says the LORD."

God desired a relationship with Israel beyond that of Awesome God and Maker of Heaven and Earth. God longed for the intimacy that He had with Adam and Eve in the garden. Sadly, it was not to be with Israel; Israel rejected the creator God to worship and follow after created things. God called it trading the fountain of living waters for broken cisterns. (Jeremiah 2:13) Talk about a bad deal!

The first hint, in the New Testament, that the Church was to be the Bride of Christ comes from John the Baptist. (Israel is not left out of being in the Bride of Christ. Paul takes care of that in Romans 7:4a, "Therefore, my brethren, you also have become dead to the law through the body of Christ, that you may be married to another—to Him who was raised from the dead....") In John 3:28–29 John the Baptist says, "You yourselves bear me witness, that I said, 'I am not the Christ,' but, 'I have been sent before Him.' He who has the bride is the bridegroom; but the friend of the bridegroom, who stands and hears him, rejoices greatly because of the bridegroom's voice. Therefore this joy of mine is fulfilled."

Jesus, Himself, continued the theme of the Church being the bride of Christ in Matthew 9:15. "And Jesus said to them, 'Can the friends of the bridegroom mourn as long as the bridegroom is with them? But the days will come when the bridegroom will be taken away from them, and then they will fast.'" And Jesus continued it in various parables, notably in Matthew 22:2 where He said: "The kingdom of heaven is like a certain king who arranged a marriage for his son...."

The subject of marriage is continued by Paul in the epistles, "For I am jealous for you with godly jealousy. For I have betrothed you to one husband, that I may present you as a chaste virgin to Christ." (2 Corinthians 11:2) Here Paul is telling us that a part of his responsibility as a minister of God is to prepare us for our marriage to Christ. Then

> *God desires a relationship with His people beyond that of Awesome God and Maker of Heaven and Earth. God longs for the intimacy that He had with Adam and Eve in the garden.*

when Paul writes in Romans 7:4b, "that you may be married to another—to Him who was raised from the dead, that we should bear fruit to God..." he is pointing out that this marriage is not to be a Platonic relationship. We are not supposed to be good friends with Jesus but hold Him at a distance. We are not talking about a physical relationship here, but an intimate relationship in our hearts with Christ whereby we are to bear Spiritual fruit unto God. We are talking about God's life flowing into our hearts and our receiving that life and being changed by the power of His life in us.

While I was writing this book, Connie McKinney, a member of our Church, shared a dream she had back in 1982. This dream was about the Bride of Christ. I was so impressed by the dream that I asked her permission to include it in my book. The following is a direct quote of Connie's dream and her interpretation as written exactly as she gave it to me. The only changes are that I embedded the Scripture references into the body of the interpretation rather than leaving them to the end.

The Bride of Jesus
(1982)

"Let us rejoice and be glad and give him glory!
For the wedding of the Lamb has come,
and his bride has made herself ready."
– Revelation 19:7

In this dream, I saw a young girl about sixteen years of age. At a glance, one could tell she had the potential of being very beautiful. But at this stage in her life, she was the picture of youthful immaturity – on the edge of adulthood and still in the process of "coming into her own". Her bright, blonde hair was bobbed in a blunt cut just beneath her ears and her teeth were covered in shiny, new braces.

This young woman stood on a green hill from which other rolling hills could be seen. All of the hills were a bright, spring green but separated by hidden valleys. On one of the distant hills, a handsome, stately young man sat upon a horse. The young girl

195

noticed he was looking at her and that his gaze never left her. He kept a watchful eye over her as if waiting and, more than this, longing for her to join him.

But she could not come, for she was not ready.

Suddenly, she sensed the presence of an older man next to her. He was fatherly in every way. He was kind, loving and concerned for her well-being. The kindly gentleman led her to a near-by stable where she was encouraged to choose a horse upon which she would ride out to meet the young man, (her future bridegroom). In some way, the young girl sensed that this older man was somehow "father" to both herself and her husband-to-be.

As she went to choose a horse, a whole host of people appeared just above her as in a mist. They too were encouraging her to prepare for her journey. There was a great sense of love, encouragement, helpfulness and rejoicing from them and the "father". They were all exuberant about the wedding to come.

INTERPRETATION:

I quickly realized that the young girl represented the Bride of Jesus, His church or Body, as she looks now. She has the potential of great beauty but is now youthful, imperfect and in the preparation stage for her wedding. Her father (God the Father) (Hebrews 2:11, Romans 8:15-17) loves her and is excited about her marriage to His Son, Jesus (the young man waiting for her in a distant place). (John 14:2-3, 1 John 3:2-3)

The people surrounding her and cheering her on were the "great cloud of witnesses", that the writer of Hebrews (Hebrews 12:1), refers to, who are ever encouraging the Christian believers to lay aside every weight and the sin which hinders their spiritual beauty from coming into full maturity (such as pictured by the young girl's bobbed hair and braces which represented signs of being molded into maturity). The saints who have gone on before us are in one accord with the Father that the "Bride" make herself ready for the time when she will join them in the great wedding celebration. I sensed no spirit of competition or selfish motive among the cloud of saints but rather a common bond of brotherly love. They wholeheartedly desire to see God's will accomplished in the "young bride" and to see her come into complete maturity.

The horses that carry and support both the Bride and Bridegroom represent the only means of transportation to all spiritual unity and maturity, that is, the Holy Spirit of God. The Bride's choosing of her horse was really a symbol of submission to the drawing power of God to work His will within her by His means and strength. In the choosing, she was giving up her own "walk" (the works of the flesh, of human strength and reasoning) in exchange for obedience to God's directives alone. (Proverbs 3:5-6)

I noticed also that the Father had helped her choose the right saddle that would hold her securely for the duration of her journey. The Father would do His part to see that she was safely brought to Jesus. (Philippians 1:6)

What impressed me the most about this dream was the total love, excitement, joy and encouragement exuding from the heart of the Father and the cloud of witnesses, in their desire to see the Bride prepare for and take her spiritual journey to Jesus. I also noticed that the present imperfections of the Bride in no way dimmed their affections for her. "While we were yet sinners, Christ died for us..." (Romans 5:8). His love is the same for us, regardless of where we are on our journey.

****

What an awesome description of God's heart for us now and His heart's desire for our future!

This bride is typified in the book and person of Esther where one of the most important events is Esther being made ready for the king. She was given twelve months of cleansing and purification then clothed in the finest apparel so that when she went in to see the king she would be pleasing to him. Let's take a closer look at this preparation.

Esther 2:12, "Each young woman's turn came to go in to King Ahasuerus after she had completed twelve months' preparation, according to the regulations for the women, for thus were the days of their preparation apportioned: six months with oil of myrrh, and six months with perfumes and preparations for beautifying (purifying KJV) women." So Esther, being among the women selected to go into the King's chamber, went through this year-long time of preparation. Esther went through both internal and external preparation. Esther 2:12 talks about perfumes (sweet odors KJV) and beautifying (purifications KJV).

> *We not only have to allow the blood of Jesus to wash away the stain of sin from our lives but to also deal with our internal motives.*

SWEET ODORS – Strong's: 1314 [besem]; spice, balsam, balsam tree, perfume; sweet, sweet smell, sweet odour.

Balsam was especially used for medicinal purposes and was taken internally. This Hebrew word was also used generically to refer to various spices.

PURIFYING – Strong's: 8562 [tamruwq]; a scraping, rubbing; remedy (for an injury).

The concept here of beautifying or purifying was expressly used for external treatments, hence the definitions of scraping and rubbing.

2 Corinthians 7:1 (NRSV), Since we have these promises, beloved, let us cleanse ourselves from every defilement of body and of spirit, making holiness perfect in the fear of God."

Acts 15:9 (NRSV) (Peter is speaking), "and in cleansing their hearts by faith he has made no distinction between them (gentiles) and us (Jews)."

1 Peter 1:22 (NRSV), Now that you have purified your souls by your obedience to the truth so that you have genuine mutual love, love one another deeply from the heart.

MYRRH MIXED WITH OLIVE OIL

Myrrh is a natural gum or resin extracted from a number of small, thorny tree species of the genus Commiphora. Myrrh resin has been used throughout history as a perfume, incense, and medicine. Myrrh mixed with wine can also be ingested. When people harvest myrrh, they wound the trees repeatedly to bleed them of the gum. If we go to Isaiah 53:4b–5 (KJV), we see the parallel between this oil of myrrh and the blood of Jesus. "Yet we esteemed Him stricken, Smitten by God, and afflicted. But He was wounded (to wound or pierce) for our transgressions (sins committed), He was bruised (OLIVE OIL comes from beating the olive branches to harvest and then crushing them to press out the oil) for our iniquities (inward tendencies to sin); The chastisement for our peace was upon Him, And by His stripes we are healed."

All cleansing from sin comes to believers by the blood of Jesus. "(B)ut if we walk in the light as he himself is in the light, we have fellowship with one another, and the blood of Jesus his Son cleanses us from all sin." (1 John 1:7 NRSV) We cannot begin to be prepared to enter the presence of the King without this first step of Salvation. We not only have to allow the blood of Jesus to wash away the stain of sin from our lives but to also deal with our internal motives.

Myrrh was a part of Jesus' life at least three distinct times. The first time was at His birth when it was a gift from the Magi along with gold and frankincense. Since myrrh was used to anoint the dead, many scholars believe this was foreshadowing Jesus' death and burial. The second time was at his death on the cross where it was offered as a drink when it was mixed with wine or vinegar. Jesus refused to drink it. The final time was at His burial when myrrh was among the spices used to embalm Jesus' body after His death. Hence, myrrh can speak to us of death to self, in other words, laying down our lives for the Gospel. In Mark 8:35 Jesus said, "For whoever desires to save his life will lose it, but whoever loses his life for My sake and the gospel's will save it." The Apostle Paul reminds us of this truth in Galatians 2:20, "I have been crucified with Christ; it is no longer I who live, but Christ lives in me; and the life which I now live in the flesh I live by faith in the Son of

God, who loved me and gave Himself for me." As God is preparing a glorious Church without spot or wrinkle we must allow the Holy Spirit to cleanse away all the old life and clothe us with the new. "Do not lie to one another, since you have put off the old man with his deeds, and have put on the new man who is renewed in knowledge according to the image of Him who created him." (Colossians 3:9–10)

The truth of our need for cleansing that we might become a glorious bride is brought out again in Ephesians 5:25-27 where Paul tells us: "Husbands, love your wives, just as Christ also loved the church and gave Himself for her, that He might sanctify and cleanse her with the washing of water by the word, that He might present her to Himself a glorious church, not having spot or wrinkle or any such thing, but that she should be holy and without blemish." Here the Apostle Paul focuses on the work that the Word does in cleansing His people. In both the Old and New Testaments God helps us to understand that there is a preparation involved with being the King's bride.

Esther 2:12 also talks about perfume or sweet odors. These sweet odors speak of sacrifice and prayer. In Psalm 141:1a & 2 David tied sacrifice and prayer together. "LORD, I cry out to You; ...Let my prayer be set before You as incense, The lifting up of my hands as the evening sacrifice." And John the Revelator said in Revelation 5:8b, "the twenty-four elders fell down before the Lamb, each having a harp, and golden bowls full of incense, which are the prayers of the saints." Our prayer life (communication/ communion) is a vital part of our growing relationship with Jesus.

In Esther we also meet Hegai the king's chamberlain. Hegai is a type of the Holy Spirit working in and through our lives. Hegai helped Esther understand what was pleasing to the King. In the New Testament Jesus gave us gifted ministries; Apostle, Prophet, Evangelist, Pastor and Teacher to help us understand what is pleasing to the King of Kings! And the Holy Spirit Himself gave us both the Fruit of the Spirit and the Gifts of the Spirit. Our growing in the knowledge and in the use of these gifts is very pleasing to our King.

Reflecting upon the Church being the Bride of Christ, consider the following Scriptures:

Revelation 19:7-8 "Let us be glad and rejoice and give Him glory, for the marriage of the Lamb has come, and His wife has made herself ready." And to her it was granted to be arrayed in fine linen, clean and bright, for the fine linen is the righteous acts of the saints.

Revelation 21:2 "Then I, John, saw the holy city, New Jerusalem, coming down out of heaven from God, prepared as a bride adorned for her husband."

No one can work hard enough to be good enough to be a part of the Bride of Christ. Ephesians 2:8–9, "For by grace you have been saved through faith, and that not of yourselves; it is the gift of God, not of works, lest anyone should boast." However, the above Scriptures from the Book of Revelation, show the cooperation of born again Christians with the working of the Holy Spirit in their lives.

Paul also shows this in Philippians 2:12–13, "Therefore, my beloved, as you have always obeyed, not as in my presence only, but now much more in my absence, work out your own salvation with fear and trembling; for it is God who works in you both to will and to do for His good pleasure." The Bride corporately making herself ready is only possible as we individually yield ourselves to and cooperate with the Holy Spirit as God works in our lives as a potter with the clay or a goldsmith purifying gold. We can hold on to the old man or we can put him off. (Ephesians 4:22, Colossians 3:9)

Here is another important Scripture about the bride. Revelation 21:9-11, "Then one of the seven angels... came to me and talked with me, saying, 'Come, I will show you the bride, the Lamb's wife.' And he carried me away in the Spirit to a great and high mountain, and showed me the great city, the holy Jerusalem, descending out of heaven from God, having the glory of God...." Isn't it awesome!

The Lamb's wife will actually have the glory of God. This glory is an imparted glory but it is the glory of God because nothing less will do for the Lamb's wife.

So, here as the time for the marriage of the Lamb draws near, we do not see a weak, anemic bride; on the contrary, we see a glorious bride fully prepared to be joined in marriage with the Son of God creator of heaven and earth! Just as the woman is the glory of the man, the Church is going to be "unto the praise of His glory." (Ephesians 1:14) God will have a bride worthy of His Son! Remember, Adam shouted out to God, "This one, this one, this one!" I believe Jesus will declare to the Father, "This one!" The Bride of Christ will truly be ready for her royal bridegroom. God is preparing a bride fit for the Son of God! The Church is that bride and she is going to be a glorious Church without spot or blemish. The Church will truly be a bride fit for a king!

Having looked at some of the glorious purposes of God for His Church and His people a very legitimate question to ask is "How can this possibly happen?" In the next chapter I will endeavor to answer that question.

> ***God is preparing a bride fit for the Son of God!***

DISCUSSION QUESTIONS FOR CHAPTER 16

Why do you think God used the analogy of Jesus as the bridegroom and the Church as His bride?

What aspects of a bridegroom do you see in Jesus?

What aspects of a bride do you see in the Church?

What did you think of the dream?

Did you get any additional insights from the dream?

How does God purify His Church both inside and out?

How do you see yourself cooperating with the Holy Spirit as He works in your life?

How can that cooperation be enhanced?

A QUICK REVIEW

As we approach the conclusion of this book, I thought it would be good to restate some of the main ideas we have covered:

- God loves us so much that He would rather die than live without us.
- God has not changed His plan; He is working through redeemed mankind to finish what He started with Adam and Eve.
- God desires a relationship with His people. He longs for the intimate fellowship that He had with Adam and Eve in the garden.
- God designed the Church to change the world.
- Jesus sent His Church on a mission and it is not just to save souls, it is also the redemption of the whole of creation.
- The Church is designed to influence the societies in which they live rather than society influencing them.
- God's Church is to be salt and light; agents of preservation and transformation in this world.
- God pours Himself into His Church so that the Church can pour Him into the world.
- We need to stop identifying with the world and begin to identify with the Glory of God.
- The symbolism of Jesus' sacrifice and redemption is found in the Tabernacle of Moses.
- The Tabernacle of Moses is a picture of our journey from sinner to mature son/daughter of God.
- Under the Old Covenant, there was an unwritten "Keep out!" sign over the curtain leading to the Holy of Holies. Under the New Covenant, there is an unwritten "Please Come In; I have been waiting for you!" sign on the now torn curtain.
- It is God's intent that even though we start out this journey as babies in Christ we do not stay there. He is transforming us into the image of His Son.
- Jesus died to wipe the record of our sins out of our lives and out of the Book of Life.
- God's indwelling presence enables believers to draw on His life and to live a new creation life, a life free from sin, every day.

- Without the giftings of the Holy Spirit no one could hope to show God's love and bring His kingdom into the world in practical ways.
- Our gifts must put the focus on God and be evidence of God's love in action.
- God's gifts are tools given by God for us to use now.
- The word *love* shows up in the Bible more than three times as often as the word *obey*.
- Obedience pleases God but doing the right thing out of a heart of love without His direct instructions brings Him delight.
- Jesus is "one-of-a-kind" and He is the "express image" of His Father.
- If we are born of God, then He is our father and our nature comes from Him.
- From the beginning God's intention has always been to make His children like Himself. Our responsibility is to choose to be conformed to His image.
- Jesus put Apostles in this world to help new believers become more like Christ as well as to influence the society in which they live.
- Everyone can prophesy through the Spirit of prophecy but not everyone who prophesies is a prophet or has the gift of prophecy.
- Jesus came to get mankind back in right relationship with God and on the right track in fulfilling God's purposes.
- A major part of God's work here on the earth is to destroy the works of the devil.
- Creation is not waiting for the coming of the Lord but for the people of God to come to their full maturity in Christ Jesus.
- We are to pray the Lord's Prayer and then be about the Father's business of subduing satan and releasing God's kingdom into the earth.
- God is preparing a bride suitable for His Son.
- God desires a Church who is purified both inside and out as a bride prepared for her husband.

NOTHING IS IMPOSSIBLE WITH GOD

As we come to the final chapter of this book, there might be some things that you see in the Word of God but can't see how they could be possible. I would like to take you to a very familiar passage of Scripture; the story of the conception and birth of Jesus, our Savior.

From Luke's account of this awesome event I would like to draw some important parallels between what happened to Mary and what is happening to us. If you haven't read the story lately, you might go to Luke 1:26-38 and read it now.

In Luke 1:28–30 we read how Mary was chosen by God, "And having come in, the angel said to her, 'Rejoice, highly favored one, the Lord is with you; blessed are you among women!' But when she saw him, she was troubled at his saying, and considered what manner of greeting this was. Then the angel said to her, 'Do not be afraid, Mary, for you have found favor with God.'" God chose this unassuming young girl for a very special purpose from among all the young women in Israel.

The Scriptures make it very plain that we also have been chosen by God. "You did not choose Me, but I chose you and appointed you that you should go and bear fruit, and that your fruit should remain, that whatever you ask the Father in My name He may give you." (John 15:16) And "... you are a chosen generation, a royal priesthood, a holy nation, His own special people, that you may proclaim the praises of Him who called you out of darkness into His marvelous light." (1 Peter 2:9) Among all the people alive in the earth today, God chose you and He chose me. God chose each of us for a specific purpose.

Mary's purpose was to birth and raise up the Son of God. Luke 1:31–33, "And behold, you will conceive in your womb and bring forth a Son, and shall call His name Jesus. He will be great, and will be called the Son of the Highest; and the Lord God will give Him the throne of His father David. And He will reign over the house of Jacob forever, and of His kingdom there will be no end."

Mary bore the literal Son of God. We, as born-again Christians, bear the image of the Son of God. Mary began to show a difference soon after conception. After all, she was pregnant and she could only hide that for a little while. When we are truly born again, our lives begin to show a difference. At new birth, we are a new creation and our outlook on life and our behavior go through a radical transformation. So much so that people should begin to notice something different about us.

> **God chose each of us for a specific purpose.**

The world misjudged Mary when they saw that she was pregnant, but it wasn't something she could hide. The world might misjudge us but we haven't been made salt and light to hide it under a bushel, etc. but to reveal it to the world. Matthew 5:14–16, "You are the light of the world. A city that is set on a hill cannot be hidden. Nor do they light a lamp and put it under a basket, but on a lampstand, and it gives light to all who are in the house. Let your light so shine before men, that they may see your good works and glorify your Father in heaven." Remember the prayer of the early Church in Jerusalem, a prayer for boldness and signs and wonders even in the midst of persecution.

What kinds of things should be different? How about showing more "love, joy, peace, longsuffering, kindness, goodness, faithfulness, gentleness, self-control" in your life? (Galatians 5:22b–23a) These are called the fruit of the Spirit for a reason; they come naturally to those who are born of the Spirit. As fallen humanity, we don't gravitate to expressing these Godly attributes naturally but as born-again Christians we should. I heard someone say it this way one time. "If someone pokes you, do you bleed vinegar or honey?" In circumstances of life both good and bad what is noticeable in your life; bitterness, anger, frustration or love, joy and peace?

Other things that should be different include the gifts of the Spirit listed in 1 Corinthians 12:8-11. As non-believers they don't show up in our lives at all but as born-again Christians we have been given several of these gifts and they can begin to operate very quickly after new birth.

When Mary heard what was to happen, she asked "How?" Luke 1:34, "Then Mary said to the angel, 'How can this be, since I do not know a man?'" You might also ask "How can this happen to me?" God's answer came quickly to Mary. Luke 1:35, "And the angel answered and said to her, 'The Holy Spirit will come upon you, and the power of the Highest will overshadow you; therefore, also, that Holy One who is to be born will be called the Son of God.'" Jesus' promise to His followers is very similar. Luke 24:49, "Behold, I send the Promise of My Father upon you; but tarry in the city of Jerusalem until you are endued with power from on high."

And it came! Acts 2:1–4 tells us, "When the Day of Pentecost had fully come, they were all with one accord in one place. And suddenly there came a sound from heaven, as of a rushing mighty wind, and it filled the whole house where they were sitting. Then there appeared to them divided tongues, as of fire, and one sat upon each of them. And they were all filled with the Holy Spirit and began to speak with other tongues, as the Spirit gave them utterance." The Holy Spirit now lives in each one of us. He is there to help us through the good times and the bad times, through times of victory and times of defeat. He has taken residence within our lives and He is there to bring to pass all of God's purposes in our lives and in His Church.

Mary began to rapidly demonstrate a supernatural lifestyle. She was carrying a baby and had not known a man. Mary was still a virgin. That is impossible in the natural but not in the supernatural workings of God. We are also supposed to demonstrate a supernatural lifestyle; just like Jesus, our Father now is God and His Spirit dwells in us and He is a supernatural God.

To encourage Mary even more, the angel told her, "Now indeed, Elizabeth your relative has also conceived a son in her old age; and this is now the sixth month for her who was called barren. For with God nothing will be impossible." (Luke 1:36-37) If something seems impossible but it is a promise from God in His Word, it is possible. For with God nothing is impossible.

Mary's response is all that it should have been and all that ours should be. Luke 1:38, "Then Mary said, 'Behold the maidservant of the Lord! Let it be to me according to your word.' And the angel departed from her." Lord, help our response to Your promises be "let it be to me according to Your word."

> *Let our response to God's promises be, "be it unto me according to Thy word." (Luke 1:38 KJV)*

The purpose of God is clear; through the Holy Spirit, we, who are in the process of being made in the image of God, are reflections of Him to the whole world. In 2 Corinthians 3:18, "But we all, with unveiled face, beholding as in a mirror the glory of the Lord, are being transformed into the same image from glory to glory, just as by the Spirit of the Lord." In Hebrews 7:24–25, "But He (Jesus), because He continues forever, has an unchangeable priesthood. Therefore He is also able to save to the uttermost (completely, perfectly, finally, and for all time and eternity - AMP) those who come to God through Him, since He always lives to make intercession for them." And in Philippians 1:6, "being confident of this very thing, that He who has begun a good work in you will complete it until the day of Jesus Christ...." We have to keep this truth close to our hearts; "With God nothing is impossible." Don't falter, don't faint, keep believing, keep pressing into all that God has and wants for us, His children. Selah!

Why do you think God choose humanity through whom to show His glory?

Why did God choose you?

When you first became a Christian, what things changed in your life?

As you have grown in the Lord, what areas of your life have you been holding on to and have not turned over to the Lord?

What is keeping you from saying, "God, let it be in me according to Your word?"

RESOURCES

Strong, J. (1995). Enhanced Strong's Lexicon. Woodside Bible Fellowship.

Swanson, J. (1997). Dictionary of Biblical Languages with Semantic Domains: Hebrew (Old Testament) (electronic ed.), Oak Harbor: Logos Research Systems, Inc.

"Discover Your God Given Gifts" by Don and Katie Fortune
www.heart2heart.org

"Tabernacle Of Moses Volumes I and II" 2001 Editions by Kelley Varner;   Printed by Tabernacle Press, Richlands, North Carolina 28574

"The Tabernacle Of Moses" by Kevin J. Conner; Copyright 1975 by Kevin J. Conner; Printed by Bible Press, Portland, Oregon 97213

HEBREW INTERLINEAR BIBLE (OT)
https://www.Scripture4all.org/OnlineInterlinear/Hebrew_Index.htm

GREEK INTERLINEAR BIBLE (NT)
https://www.Scripture4all.org/OnlineInterlinear/Greek_Index.htm

"AN EXPOSITORY DICTIONARY OF NEW TESTAMENT WORDS" by W. E. Vine, M.A. Fleming H. Revell Company, Old Tappan, New Jersey; first published 1940

"All May Prophesy – Understanding Prophecy" by Roy Ralph; Available on Amazon.com

Random House Kernerman Webster's College Dictionary, (© 2010 by Random House, Inc. All rights reserved.)

Logos Bible Software 8.11 Copyright 2000-2010 Faithlife Corporation